NUMERICAL ABILITY FOR 11+

11+ NUMERACY WORKBOOK 2

Fully classroom-tested by Teachitright pupils and approved by parents

- Statistics

- Data Handling and Interpretation

- Shape and Space

Teachitright
Learn. Develop. Succeed.

UBP
University of Buckingham Press

Copyright information

Billy the Bookworm™ is the property of Teachitright

Authors

Chris Pearse

Jessica Hodge

The authors have asserted their moral rights under the Copyright, Designs and Patents Act, 1988, to be identified as the authors of this work.

First published in Great Britain in 2017 by

The University of Buckingham Press
Yeomanry House
Hunter Street
Buckingham MK18 1EG

A CIP catalogue record for this book is available at the British Library

ISBN 9781908684738

Teachitright

Teachitright is one of the most successful 11+ tuition companies in the South East. In the last 10 years we've supported thousands of pupils for both grammar school and independent school entry. We have 11 tuition centres across Buckinghamshire, Berkshire and Surrey.

Based on our wealth of experience and knowledge, we have produced a range of books that will help support your child through their 11+ journey in both CEM style and traditional 11+ tests and many Common Entrance exams. Our books, written by qualified teachers, have been classroom tested with pupils and adapted to ensure children are fully prepared and able to perform to the best of their ability.

Our unique mascot, Billy the Bookworm, will help guide children through the book and gives helpful hints and tips throughout.

We hope you find this book very useful and informative and wish you luck on your 11+ journey.

Teachitright holds a number of comprehensive revision courses and mock exams throughout the year. If you would like to find out more information, please visit:

www.teachitright.com

This Numerical Ability Workbook 2 alongside Workbook 1 provides the perfect preparation for both 11+ and Common Entrance exams. This book contains data handling, shape and space and statistics. Workbook 1 contains the key topics working with numbers, equivalent values and algebraic calculations.

How to use this book
As this book is broken down into **lessons** that cover different topics, it can be used to focus on individual areas of development or to work through every mathematical topic.

Learn: An informative teaching section to help with the key points and techniques for that lesson topic. It includes worked examples.

Develop: Opportunity to practise short calculations based on the lesson topic to ensure key principles and techniques are fully understood.

Timed tests: Strategically placed progressive timed tests to help build confidence with worded problems and time management.

The **answer section** gives detailed explanations to aid revision. There is also a **glossary** on page 68. It is important for the pupil to understand and learn keywords and phrases that are likely to appear in the exam.

In the back of the book is a **marking chart** and **progress grid** to help track your child's development throughout the topics and to highlight strengths and weaknesses.

CONTENTS

Page 6

SECTION 1:
STATISTICS

Look out for Billy's tips and hints.

LEARN

In the first section of this book you will be learning about statistics, that is different ways of analysing data in large quantities. There are four lessons and the first one is on Ratio and Proportion.

Ratios

Ratios demonstrate the **relationship between two numbers** and how they compare to one another. Examples of ratios can be seen in many everyday situations, for instance when mixing up squash. If it states on the bottle 1 part squash to 4 parts water, it is important to add the correct quantities.

We often represent ratios as two numbers with a colon in between, for example 3:4

For example: The diagram below has a ratio of 3:4 and means 3 to every 4. For every 3 red squares there are 4 blue triangles. When something is shared in a ratio you first add up the numbers in the given ratio to find out how many equal parts you need. In the above ratio this would mean adding 3 + 4 together to equal 7. In the example about squash above, there are 5 parts in total (1 + 4).

So, if you see the following sign outside the cinema it can be represented as 1:2

1 FREE child cinema ticket 'to every' 2 adult cinema tickets

To find an equivalent ratio you must multiply or divide both sides by the same number. Therefore, if we use the cinema ticket scenario again, if you had 4 adults going to watch the film you're entitled to 2 FREE child tickets.

2:4 = 2 free child tickets to every 4 adult tickets.

4:8 = 4 free child tickets to every 8 adult tickets.

LEARN

Sometimes ratios can be shown with more than two numbers. For example, if we had a concrete mix containing cement, sand and stones, a typical mix might be in a ratio of 1:2:6. For every set quantity of cement, you require double the amount of sand and six times the amount of stones.

Proportion

A proportion of something is a way of describing **a part of a whole**. You can find the word proportion in everyday situations. For example, if you bake a cake, quantities in the recipe are increased in proportion if a bigger cake is needed.

 $$\frac{1}{3} = \frac{2}{6}$$

Two quantities are in direct proportion when they increase or decrease in the same ratios. For example, if there are 4 boys to every 3 girls in a class, the proportion of 8 boys to every 6 girls would be the same. The two ratios are the same, 4:3 and 8:6 but the first is written in the simplest form.

An example of a proportion style question:

If 12 pencils cost 60p. How much would 15 pencils cost?

First, work out the cost of one pencil, which is 60 ÷ 12 = 5p. Then, to find the cost of 15 pencils, multiply 15 by 5. This equals 75p.

DEVELOP

Write these questions using the correct ratio symbol.

1)   3 oranges were eaten to every 5 pears

2)   On a necklace there were 6 emeralds to every 4 rubies

3)   In a suitcase there were 7 socks to every 2 t-shirts packed

4)   1cm on a map represents 50km in real life

5)   10 footballs were kicked at the goal to every 3 saved

Write the following ratios in their simplest form

6)   48:16

7)   72:18

8)   56:49

9)   108:84

10)   250:1000

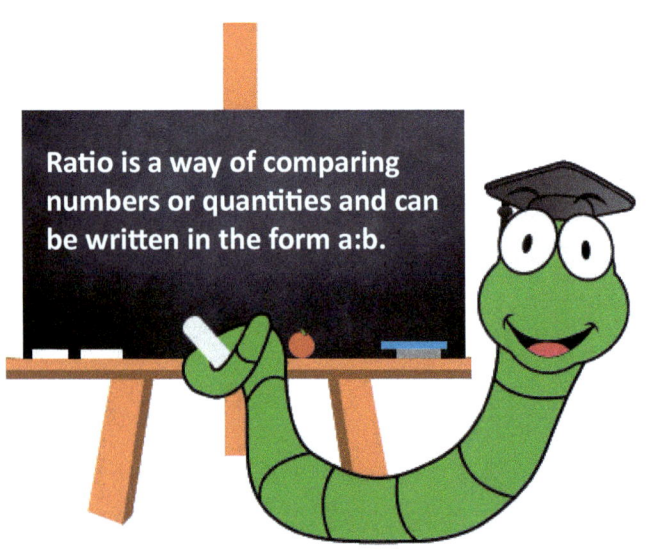

Ratio is a way of comparing numbers or quantities and can be written in the form a:b.

TIMED TEST   15 MINS

Circle the letter above the correct answer with a pencil.

1) £2.40 is shared between Jessica, Daisy and Olivia in the ratio 3:2:1. How much does Daisy receive?

A	B	C	D	E
40p	80p	£1.20	£1.60	20p

2) A bag of sweets is shared between Arzaan, Rory and Finley in the ratio of 5:3:1. There are 54 sweets. How many does Arzaan receive?

A	B	C	D	E
60	6	18	30	24

3) Arran and Kushi win £1000 between them. They agree to divide the money in the ratio 2:3. How much does Kushi receive?

A	B	C	D	E
£200	£400	£600	£800	£750

4) A necklace is made with silver and gold beads in the ratio of 7:3. There are 90 beads in the necklace. How many are silver?

A	B	C	D	E
27	45	64	54	63

5) On a map the scale is 1cm = 100km. What would the distance in metres be if 5 centimetres were used on the map?

A	B	C	D	E
500000m	50000m	5000m	500m	50m

6) An orange is divided in the ratio 4:2:1. If there are 14 segments, how many pieces represent the largest share?

A	B	C	D	E
2	6	7	8	4

7) A pack of 52 playing cards were dealt out in the ratio 7:4:2. How many cards are in the smallest proportion?

A	B	C	D	E
9	8	16	28	13

8) At a party 108 biscuits were shared in the ratio 2:3:1. How many biscuits did the group who had 2 parts receive?

A	B	C	D	E
18	54	36	18	90

9) In a cricket test series, the runs scored by Freddie, Jimmy and Joe were shared in a ratio of 3:2:2. If 560 runs were scored, how many runs did Freddie score?

A	B	C	D	E
160	320	250	400	240

10) In a school car park the colours of the vehicles were green, red, silver, black and blue. The car park had 55 cars in the ratio 1:4:2:1:3. How many red cars were in the car park?

A	B	C	D	E
15	20	25	5	48

11) A model train is made to a scale of 1:30. This means every 1cm represents 30cm. Therefore, how long in metres would a model train be if it measured 5cm?

A	B	C	D	E
150cm	1.3m	1.50m	30m	50m

12) Granny Grace divided 144 sweets between her grandchildren in the ratio of 1:2:3:4:1:1 due to their age. What was the greatest proportion of sweets received by one of her grandchildren?

A	B	C	D	E
48	24	60	12	72

13) A moorland map is drawn to a scale of 1cm = 9km. A distance of 7.5cm on the map represents how many kilometres of the moor?

A	B	C	D	E
65.5km	63.5km	66.5km	67.5km	68.5km

14) At a fairground 240 litres of pineapple squash was made up in the ratio 3:5, 3 parts pineapple squash and 5 parts water. How much water was added?

A	B	C	D	E
90L	150L	120L	180L	130L

15) Kajol has a bag of 70 sweets. She keeps 10 for herself and gives ⅓ of the remaining sweets to her brother Rajan. The rest of the sweets are shared between Kajol's Dad and Mum in a ratio of 6:2. How many sweets does Dad receive?

A	B	C	D	E
40	20	60	30	50

Page 13

LEARN

Probability is the **likelihood or chance** of something happening. In our everyday language we use probability terms like certain, unlikely or improbable. One common situation when we describe the chance of something happening is the weather.

'There is an unlikely chance it will rain today in the south-east'

You can use fractions, decimals or percentages to describe probability. This useful probability scale helps you understand the relationship between these different areas of maths.

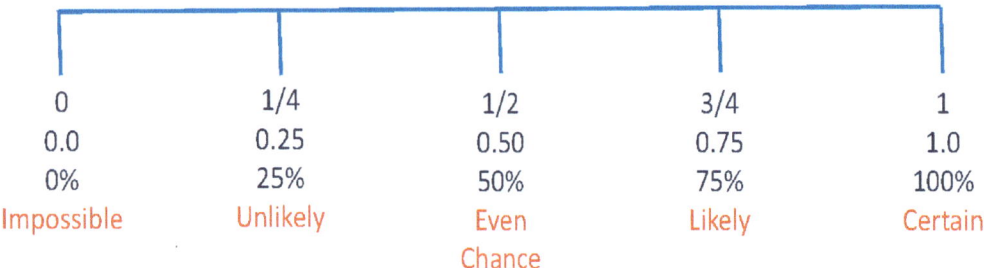

0	1/4	1/2	3/4	1
0.0	0.25	0.50	0.75	1.0
0%	25%	50%	75%	100%
Impossible	Unlikely	Even Chance	Likely	Certain

When you are solving probability questions you need to consider the number of possible outcomes. For example, if you roll a dice you could get 1, 2, 3, 4, 5 or 6. These are referred to as outcomes. There is an equal chance of rolling any of these numbers (outcomes).

So, if you throw two dice, what is the probability of getting a 6 on both dice? When you roll two dice, there are now 36 different and unique ways the dice can fall. This figure is arrived at by multiplying the number of ways the first dice can fall (six) by the number of ways the second dice can come up (six). $6 \times 6 = 36$. Therefore, there is a 1 in 36 ($\frac{1}{36}$) chance of rolling two 6s on two dice.

The probability of an outcome = $\dfrac{\text{number of ways the outcome could happen}}{\text{total number of possible outcomes}}$

DEVELOP

Find the probability of the following events.

1) The likelihood of rolling a prime number on a dice.

2) Choosing a red pencil from a pack of 2 blue, 3 green, 4 yellow and 3 red.

3) The chance of three coins all landing on tails.

4) Choosing a day of the week at random.

5) Out of the numbers 1 to 10 choosing a squared number.

Answer the following probability questions based on this spinner. Give answers as a fraction.

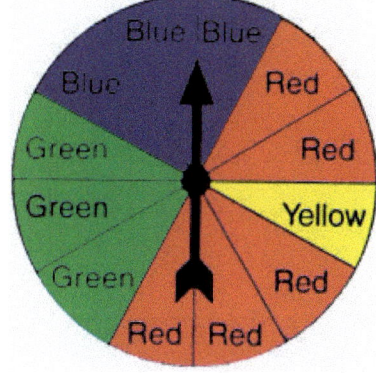

6) What is the likelihood of getting a red on the spinner?

7) What is the chance of getting a yellow on the spinner?

8) What is the chance of getting a blue or a green colour?

9) What is the likelihood of landing on any colour except blue?

10) What is the chance of getting any colour except yellow?

You can often use a probability scale. 1 is certain and 0 is impossible.

TIMED TEST 15 MINS

In a bag there are 5 white balls, 2 green balls and 1 red ball.

1) What is the probability of picking out a red or a white ball?

A	B	C	D	E
$\frac{1}{4}$	$\frac{1}{2}$	$\frac{5}{8}$	$\frac{3}{4}$	$\frac{7}{8}$

2) If one white ball is removed, what is the chance of picking out a white ball?

A	B	C	D	E
$\frac{2}{8}$	$\frac{3}{8}$	$\frac{4}{7}$	$\frac{1}{2}$	$\frac{2}{7}$

A pack of 52 cards contains suits of clubs, hearts, diamonds and spades. There are 4 Aces, 4 Kings, 4 Queens and 4 Jacks in each pack.

3) What is the probability of picking out an ace?

A	B	C	D	E
$\frac{1}{13}$	$\frac{1}{5}$	$\frac{2}{13}$	$\frac{1}{7}$	$\frac{4}{26}$

4) What is the likelihood of selecting a picture card (Jack, Queen or King)?

A	B	C	D	E
$\frac{16}{52}$	$\frac{20}{52}$	$\frac{32}{50}$	$\frac{12}{52}$	$\frac{36}{52}$

5) What is the probability that you will pick a King of Diamonds?

A	B	C	D	E
$\frac{4}{52}$	$\frac{13}{52}$	$\frac{1}{52}$	$\frac{6}{52}$	$\frac{3}{52}$

Katie's CD player is on the random choice option. There are 15 songs in total – 6 pop songs, 3 slow songs, 4 hip hops songs and 2 house tunes.

6) What is the probability of the song being either a slow song or a house tune?

A	B	C	D	E
$\frac{5}{12}$	$\frac{1}{3}$	$\frac{6}{15}$	$\frac{1}{4}$	$\frac{6}{15}$

7) What is the likelihood of the song not being hip hop?

A	B	C	D	E
$\frac{6}{15}$	$\frac{1}{2}$	$\frac{4}{15}$	$\frac{9}{15}$	$\frac{11}{15}$

In the school's pencil box there were 5 red pencils, 2 blue pencils, 8 yellow pencils, 15 black pencils and 6 green pencils. When the box was new there were 50 pencils.

8) What is the probability of picking out a blue pencil at random?

A	B	C	D	E
$\frac{2}{50}$	$\frac{1}{25}$	$\frac{2}{34}$	$\frac{1}{18}$	$\frac{4}{36}$

9) What is the likelihood of choosing a red or blue pencil out of the box?

A	B	C	D	E
$\frac{7}{50}$	$\frac{7}{36}$	$\frac{1}{4}$	$\frac{1}{6}$	$\frac{5}{36}$

10) If 10 black pencils were lost out of the box, what is the new probability of a green pencil being chosen at random in its lowest form?

A	B	C	D	E
$\frac{6}{26}$	$\frac{6}{50}$	$\frac{3}{25}$	$\frac{6}{40}$	$\frac{3}{13}$

11) A company makes calculators. The company knows that the probability that a calculator will be defective is $\frac{1}{20}$. If a box contains 1000 calculators, how many are likely to be defective?

A	B	C	D	E
50	750	20	40	100

12) A bag holds 1 yellow and 4 green balls. A ball is taken out from the bag and is not replaced. Another ball is then taken out at random. If the first ball taken out is yellow, what is the probability that the second ball taken out is green?

A	B	C	D
probable	unlikely	certain	likely

13) A box of chocolates contains milk and dark chocolates. The chance of getting a milk chocolate is $\frac{5}{36}$. What is the probability of getting a dark chocolate?

A	B	C	D	E
$\frac{4}{6}$	$\frac{28}{26}$	$\frac{31}{36}$	$\frac{5}{6}$	$\frac{11}{12}$

14) If three coins are thrown what is the probability of two coins landing heads up?

A	B	C	D	E
$\frac{1}{8}$	$\frac{1}{3}$	$\frac{1}{2}$	$\frac{2}{3}$	$\frac{1}{4}$

15) If four dice are thrown at once, what is the probability of throwing 4 ones?

A	B	C	D	E
$\frac{1}{4}$	$\frac{1}{1296}$	$\frac{1}{1210}$	$\frac{4}{1296}$	$\frac{1}{36}$

LEARN

Finding averages and a range are often tested in an 11+ exam. Let's check you know what each type of average and the range means. There are three different types of averages of a set of data: **mean**, the **median** and the **mode**.

Mean (or average): Add together the numbers in the set of data and divide the total by how many numbers are in the set.

Example one: Working out the mean
In a mental arithmetic test, a group of pupils got these marks:
21, 22, 19, 18, 20

The total is 100 and there are 5 marks. Therefore, the mean is 100 ÷ 5 = 20

Median: The median is the middle number. To find this you need to reorder the numbers in the set in order of size. Find the middle number. If there are two middle numbers, you have to add those two numbers together and divide by 2.

Example two: Working out the median
Below is the number of miles driven each day by an electrician:
18, 3, 24, 16, 17, 23, 9

The data set reordered is:
3, 9, 16, 17, 18, 23, 24
17 is the median number.

Mode: To find this type of average you discover the number which appears the most frequently in the set of data.

Example three: Working out the mode
A set of temperatures recorded in one week in Maidenhead were:
16, 15, 14, 13, 15, 14, 14

14 is the modal number as it appears most often.

Range: To find the range of a set of data, simply find the difference between the smallest number and the largest number.

Example four: Finding the range
Results of a science exam taken in Year 6:
65, 72, 32, 89, 78, 56, 61

The smallest number is 32
The largest number is 89
The range is the difference between 89 and 32

57 is the range.

DEVELOP

Below are the marks awarded for a maths mental arithmetic test out of 25.

11, 8, 20, 14, 17, 20

1)   What is the mode?

2)   What is the mean?

3)   What is the range?

4)   What is the average?

5)   What is the median number?

TIMED TEST   15 MINS

1) Ankush enjoys running and he keeps a diary of his distances covered. These are the distances over a six-week period.

    | 4.5km | 3.5km | 5km | 6.5km | 4.5km | 6km |

    What is the average distance travelled per week?

A	B	C	D	E
5.5km	6km	7.5km	6.5km	5km

2) In a kitchen cupboard the following volumes were recorded on different food cans and bottles.

    | 650ml | 800ml | 300ml | 200ml | 50ml |

    What is the mean?

A	B	C	D	E
500ml	200ml	300ml	400ml	150ml

3) The masses of John's pets are listed below.

    | 20kg | 8kg | 200g | 800g | 1kg | 6kg |

    What is the average?

A	B	C	D	E
6kg	5kg	700g	8kg	900g

4) A shop sells 14 blue, 32 green, 12 white, 47 black and 17 red coats.
    What is the median?

A	B	C	D	E
47	32	14	12	17

5) Oli received the following amounts of pocket money for helping around the house.

    | £2.80 | £3.25 | £2.50 | £4.75 | £1.25 |

    What is the range?

A	B	C	D	E
£3.25	£4.00	£3.50	£4.25	£4.50

6) Five television programmes last for different lengths of time.

    | 35 minutes | 45 minutes | 90 minutes | 60 minutes | 30 minutes |

    What is the average?

A	B	C	D	E
62 minutes	56 minutes	52 minutes	60 minutes	30 minutes

7) In a shop, DVDs cost the following amounts.

    £4.24   £3.99   £1.98   £1.79   £3

    What is the mean?

A	B	C	D	E
£3	£4	£5.50	£6.50	£3.99

8) What is the median from the five buildings in a high street that measure the following?

    1050ft   980ft   1020ft   870ft   1010ft

A	B	C	D	E
980ft	1050ft	1020ft	1010ft	870ft

9) At a huge pop concert, the following amount of tickets were sold for different days.

    20000   35000   25000   39000   31000

    What is the average?

A	B	C	D	E
40000	25000	30000	45000	20000

10) On five separate days in London the temperatures were:

    −2°C   10°C   21°C   −7°C   11°C

    What is the range?

A	B	C	D	E
8°C	28°C	17°C	12°C	18°C

11) The total mass of seven rugby players is 630kg. What is the average mass?

A	B	C	D	E
100kg	70kg	90kg	110kg	80kg

12) A diver recorded the following temperatures in the water

    8, −7, 5, −5, 6, −1, 0, 2, 6, 8, 8, 9

    What is the median?

A	B	C	D	E
5	5.5	6	7	4

13) What is the mean of the following number of pages in books:

    227, 103, 258, 386 and 441?

A	B	C	D	E
227	238	258	283	328

14) Jane spent the following amounts in her local post office: £3.02, £5.76, £4.43, £5.23, £6.70, £1.39. What is the range?

A	B	C	D	E
£5.31	£5.21	£5.41	£5.32	£5.33

15) The mean of five numbers is 180. Four of the numbers are 155, 162, 190, and 198. What is the fifth number?

A	B	C	D	E
190	180	175	195	185

LEARN

In this topic you will learn about **converting units of measurement and units of time**. Conversion is a topic where many pupils get very confused. It is a topic which often appears in maths exams as well as in everyday life so it is important that you can convert confidently.

Conversion of units of measurement
There are two systems of measurement which continue to be used. They are:

1) The metric system, which is most commonly used in the UK and other parts of Europe
2) The imperial system, which is more traditional, is mainly used in parts of Africa, Asia and America as well as on a more reduced level now in the UK.

Tables 1 and 2 show the different units of mass (weight), length (distance) and volume (capacity) and Table 3 shows a comparison of both.

Table 1: Metric system

Length	Weight	Capacity
10mm = 1cm	1000mg = 1g	1000ml = 1 litre
100cm = 1m	1000g = 1kg	100cl = 1 litre
1000m = 1km	1000kg = 1 tonne	1000cm^3 = 1 litre

Table 2: Imperial system

12 inches =	1 foot
3 feet =	1 yard
16 ounces =	1 pound
14 pounds =	1 stone
8 pints =	1 gallon
⅖ hectare =	1 acre

Table 3: Metric units to imperial units (approx.)

0.91m =	1 yard
1.6km =	1 miles
1m =	39 inches
30cm =	1 foot
2.5cm =	1 inch
1kg =	2.2 pounds
25g =	1 ounce
1 litre =	1.75 pints
4.5 litres =	1 gallon

LEARN

Time conversion

It is also important to have a good knowledge on how to convert between different time periods. Below is a useful table to help you.

Table 4

60 seconds =	1 minute
60 minutes =	1 hour
24 hours =	1 day
7 days =	1 week
52 weeks =	1 year
12 months =	1 year
10 years =	1 decade
100 years =	1 century

K refers to kilo which is associated with 1000
C refers to cent which is associated with 100

How to apply conversion to the metric system

It is important to know how to multiply and divide by 10, 100 and 1000 as, in the metric system of measurement, the units are related to their sub-units (km to m to cm to mm) by powers of 10. More information on powers of 10 can be found in Workbook 1.

If you are converting from a large known unit to a smaller unit you have to multiply.
For example, 3 kilometres converted to metres is 3000 metres.

If you are converting from a small known unit to a large unit you have to divide.
For example, 2000 grams converted to kilograms is 2 kilograms.

kg to g	convert		inverse		
3kg	3 × 1000	3000g	3000g	3000 ÷ 1000	3kg
km to m					
2km	2 × 1000	2000m	2000m	2000 ÷ 1000	2km
L to ml					
4L	4 × 1000	4000ml	4000ml	4000 ÷ 1000	4L
m to cm					
8m	8 × 100	800cm	800cm	800 ÷ 100	8m
cm to mm					
5cm	5 × 10	50mm	50mm	50 ÷ 10	5cm

To convert 5cm to mm = 5 × 10 = 50mm;
inverse convert 50mm to cm = 50 ÷ 10 = 5cm.

DEVELOP

Metric conversion

1) Convert 384m to cm =

2) How many kgs are in 9800g?

3) Convert 27300ml to litres =

4) How many cm are in 8m?

5) Convert 98cm to mm =

6) How many m in 9.7km?

7) Convert 0.7L to ml =

8) How many g are in 0.07kg?

9) Convert 420mm to cm =

10) How many mm are in 7m?

Time conversion

11) Convert 9 years to months =

12) How many years are in 18 centuries?

13) Convert 1440 seconds to minutes =

14) How many years are in 12 decades?

15) How many years equates to 7 millennia?

16) Convert 7 hours to minutes =

17) How many seconds are in 10 hours?

18) Convert the month of July to hours =

19) How many seconds is 3.5 hours?

20) Convert 8 years to days =

TIMED TEST   *15 MINS*

1) A glass holds 50ml of juice. How many glasses can Jovan fill from six 1 litre bottles?

A	B	C	D	E
80	120	20	60	12

2) It took Lara three weeks to complete her history project. She worked on it for four hours a night. How many minutes, in total, did it take her to complete the project?

A	B	C	D	E
4050 mins	5000 mins	84 mins	3000 mins	5040 mins

3) The average length of a car is 3.5 metres. If there are 3000 cars in a bumper-to-bumper traffic jam, determine the length of the queue in kilometres.

A	B	C	D	E
10.5km	10km	15km	300km	35km

4) Jess and Neil are celebrating their Silver Wedding Anniversary this year. This is equivalent to 25 full years of marriage. On the actual time of their anniversary, how many hours would they have they been married?

A	B	C	D	E
91250 hrs	190000 hrs	219144 hrs	9125 hrs	219000 hrs

5) There is a cycling competition organised between schools in Year 6. Pinak decides to enter. He travels 4 metres every second. How far will he travel, in kilometres, in 20 minutes?

A	B	C	D	E
2.4km	24km	3km	4.2km	4.8km

6) It took a total of three and a half full days to prepare for John and Myra's Diamond Wedding banquet. How many minutes, in total, was this?

A	B	C	D	E
5040 mins	84 mins	3500 mins	5300 mns	405 mins

7) Sam bought 10 tins of nails which come in one box. The box weighed 15kg. What is the mass, in grams, of each tin of nails?

A	B	C	D	E
1000g	1500g	1.5g	15g	15000g

8) Helen decides to enter for a junior triathlon. She has to run for 240000cm, swim for 800m and cycle for 3.5km. What is the total distance, in kilometres, Helen has to cover?

A	B	C	D	E
6.9km	6.53km	6.7km	65km	6.5km

9) It is Wednesday, and Ishleen attends the lunch-time science club. The topic today is dissolving salt. The teacher divides four 1.5kg bags of salt evenly between 15 club members. How many kilograms has Ishleen been given?

A	B	C	D	E
0.4kg	0.5kg	40kg	4kg	5kg

10) Krish was decorating his bedroom. He required a range of paint colours. In total he used 4.75 litres of paint. How much, in ml, did he use?

A	B	C	D	E
4570ml	4750ml	475ml	457ml	45.7ml

11) It took Kevin 25 minutes to walk home from school. How long did it take him in seconds?

A	B	C	D	E
15000	180	1500	150	1800

12) Neil bought four 17kg bags of dog food on a special promotion for his two dogs, Molly and 'Boy'. How much in grams, did he buy?

A	B	C	D	E
6800g	17000g	6500g	68000g	12000g

13) In Miriam's maths lesson, she was taught how to convert imperial measurement to metric. If 1 yard is equal to 0.91 metres, what distance, in metres, is her maths class room to the dining hall at school, if she measures 236 yards?

A	B	C	D	E
217.64m	214.76m	387.95m	236.09m	91.23m

14) Trevor filled his car with 15 gallons of petrol. It cost him £1.08 per litre. If the conversion rate is 1 gallon to 4.5 litres, how much did it cost, in pounds, for Trevor to fill his car?

A	B	C	D	E
£79.20	£72.09	£67.50	£72.90	£21.48

15) James's school field has an area of 15 acres. His task was to find the conversion rate from acres to hectares and tell the class the equivalent size of the field, in hectares. He read that 1 acre is equal to ⅖ hectare. With this in mind, how many hectares is the area of James's school field?

A	B	C	D	E
9	3	7	8	6

SECTION 2:
DATA HANDLING AND INTERPRETATION

LEARN

Data is a piece of information, normally referring to a set of values, that can be collected, analysed and plotted, or 'handled' (illustrated) in some form such as on a line graph, bar chart or pie chart. From observing what is shown on the graph, for example, conclusions, or 'interpretations' can be made. It is important to read and look carefully, with as much accuracy as possible, as your interpretations will help you to answer the questions correctly.

How would you, or other people, in your class answer these questions?

- How many brothers or sisters do you have?

- How do you travel to school?

- What pets do you have?

- What is your favourite colour?

Such individual answers may be interesting to know but would be far more fascinating if you were to compare your answers to everyone else's in the class. This is why it is important how you 'handle' such data and look at comparisons and therefore draw your own conclusion, or interpretation, to each question. For example, a dog may be the most common pet or blue could be the most popular, favourite colour.

Normally, in the exams, you would be asked to interpret the information shown and not to construct a graph (mainly due to limited time).

LEARN

There are two types of data:

Discreet data (or grouped) data is referring to data that can be counted. The data includes values which are distinct or separate such as the number of puppies in a litter. This information is often shown in the form of a bar chart or pie chart.

Continuous data is data that is obtained by measuring. It can take on any value, such as temperature, mass, height and rainfall. Such data is often shown in the form of a line graph.

Bar charts
A bar chart is often used to compare numbers, or frequency, of occurrences. It can be used to show both discreet and continuous data. It is made up of bars or columns in equal width. The bars can be drawn with or without gaps between and their height normally refers to the frequency of occurrences.

Example one: Bar charts and frequency charts
Now we will go through the process of drawing a bar chart from discreet data which has been tabulated on a **frequency chart** (Table 1).

Table 1: A frequency chart to show the number of house points collected in the autumn term by Year 6 children

Number of house points	Number of children (frequency)
1–10	8
11–20	12
21–30	33
31–40	28
41–50	10

From Table 1 you can see the groups are separated (1 to 10, 11 to 20, etc).

If you are asked to draw a bar chart you don't need to add up all the children. Instead look at the highest number in the frequency column. In this example it is 33 children. Then decide on the intervals for the vertical axis of the bar chart. These have to be equal intervals so that the length of the bar can be used to represent the frequency. Then draw on the bars for each of the frequency columns.

LEARN

Bar chart 1: Illustrating Table 1 data

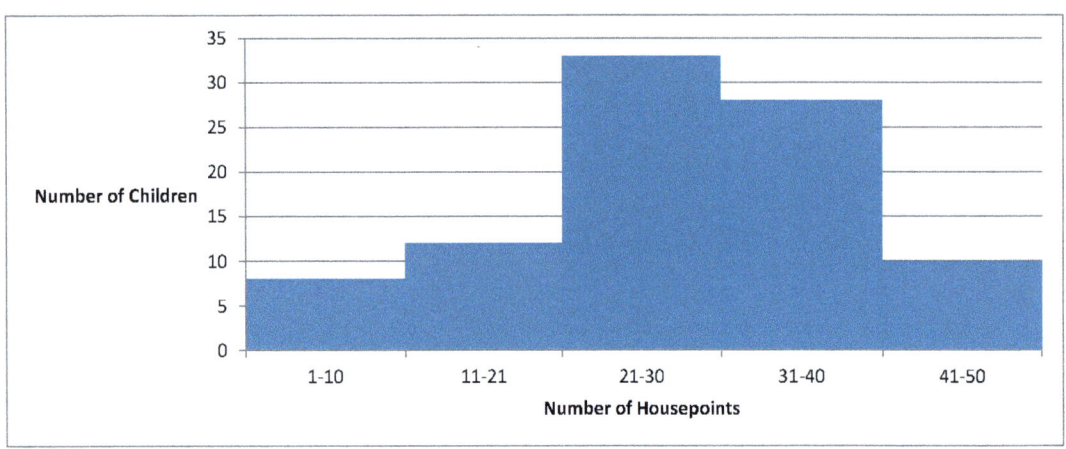

Example two: Bar charts with continuous data and tally charts
Now let's look at drawing a bar chart with continuous data tabulated on a **tally chart** (Table 2).

Table 2: A tally chart to show the amount of money raised in a sponsored readathon by Year 5 children.

Money raised (£000)	Number of children	Frequency
0≤ × <10	|||| ||||	10
10≤ × <20	|||| |||| |||| |||| ||||	25
20≤ × <30	|||| |||| |||| |||| |||| |||	28
30≤ × <40	|||| |||| |||	13
40≤ × <50	|||| |||| ||||	15

In Table 2 you can see that the groups are continuous, as shown in the money column.

10≤ × <20
This means the data is equal to or more than 10 and less than 20. Data shown in this way prevents any separation and allows continuation.

LEARN

Bar chart 2: Illustrating Table 2 data

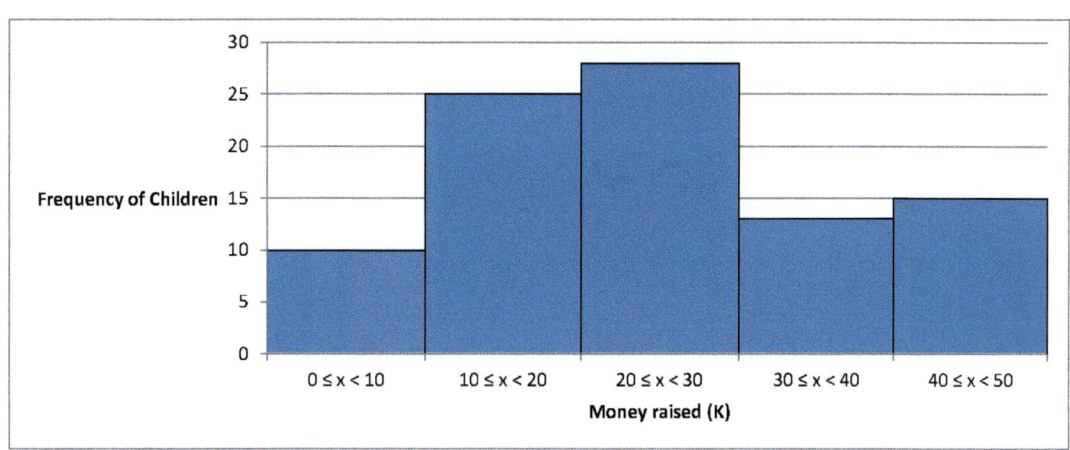

There are also other types of bar charts about which you may need to answer questions in the exam or everyday life, so it is good to be able to recognise as many as possible.

A = Comparative, or dual bar charts
B = Horizontal bar charts
C = Standard bar charts
D = Composite bar charts – demonstrates multiple data points
E = 3D horizontal bar charts

A

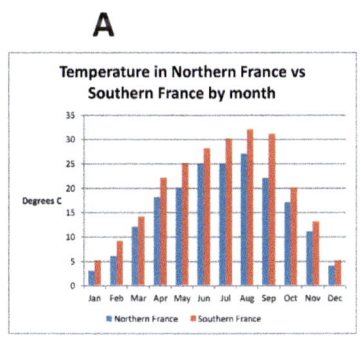

B

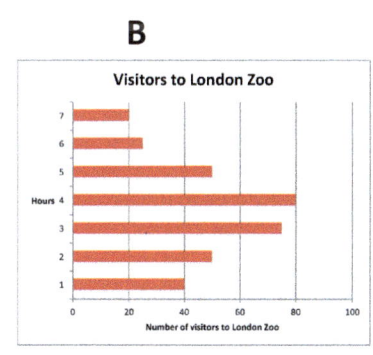

C

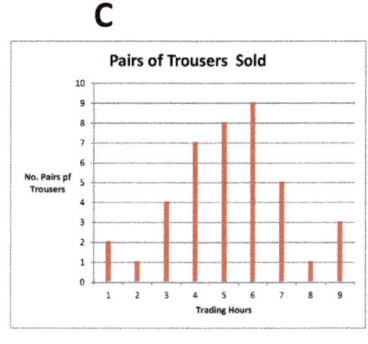

D

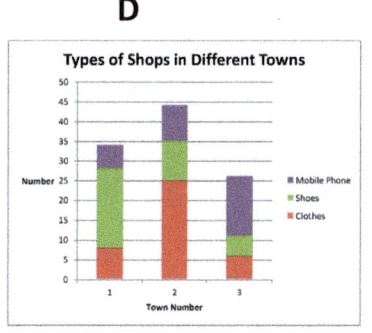

E

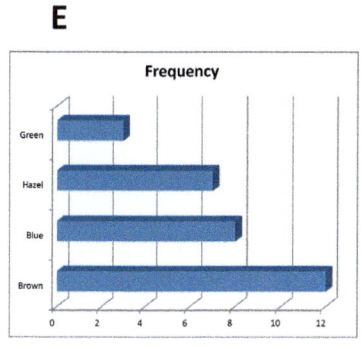

DEVELOP

See if you can answer the questions below.

Look at the composite (stacked) bar chart below and answer the following questions:

A)   How many shops in total, were surveyed?

B)   How many mobile phone shops in total were there?

C)   Which town has the least number of shoe shops?

D)   How many more shoe shops are in town 1 than in town 3?

E)   Work out the combined number of shoe shops and clothes shops in towns 2 and 3.

LEARN

A line graph shows **a line joining a set of points**. The points represent the relationship between two variables, such as distance and time.

Line graphs normally display **continuous data**, and have a vertical and a horizontal axis. This line graph demonstrates the daily hours of sunshine in a week, with the 'number of hours of sunshine' on the vertical axis and the 'days of the week' on the horizontal axis.

Line graph 1

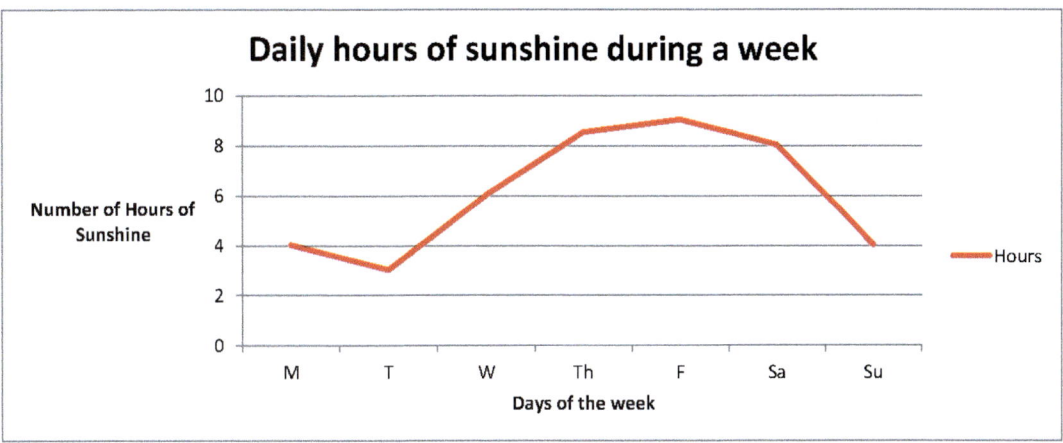

There are also other types of line graph including horizontal and vertical bar line charts. Below are some more examples.

A

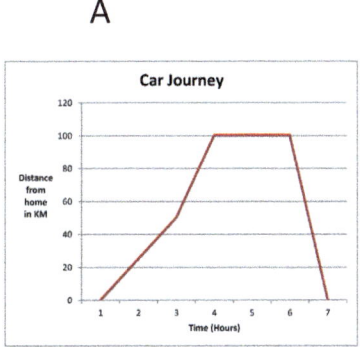

B

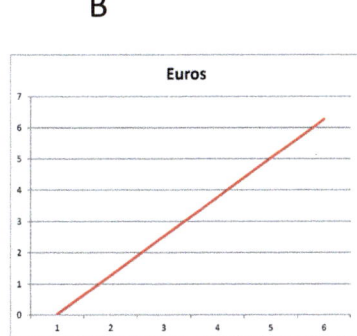

LEARN

C

Duration of stay of visitors to Whipsnade Zoo over one day

D

Number of pairs of Trousers sold in a shop in each hour of trading

1)   Journey tracking chart

2)   Conversion chart

3)   Horizontal bar line chart

4)   Vertical bar line chart

DEVELOP

Answer the following questions about the line graph below.

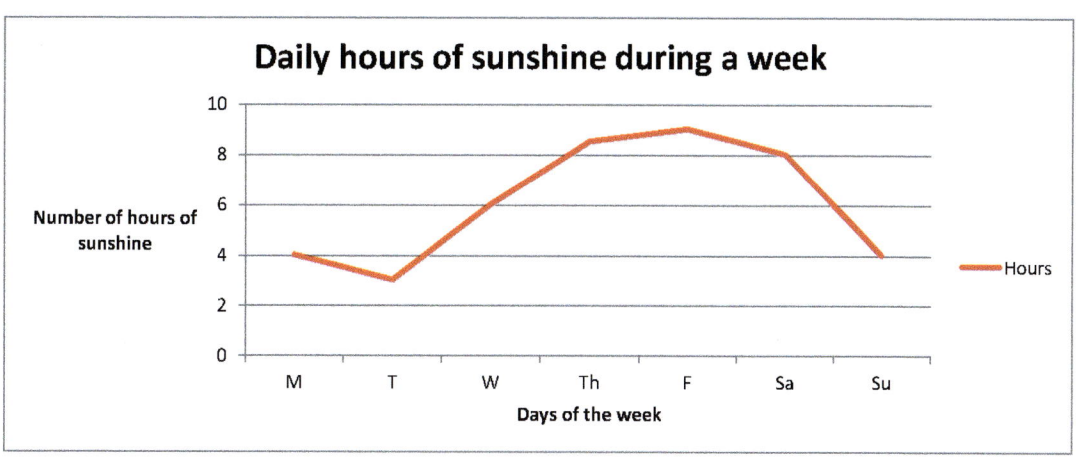

Daily hours of sunshine during a week

(The answer is directly above the letter of the day of the week)

1)   On which day were the most hours of sunshine recorded?

2)   Which two days had the same number of sunshine hours?

3)   Which day showed the least number of hours' sunshine?

4)   What was the total number of hours of sunshine in the week?

5)   What was the range in hours of sunshine during the week?

LEARN

As well as bar charts and line graphs there are a number of other ways to display data visually, for example pie charts, pictograms and Venn diagrams. They can display different sets of data in different ways and in this lesson you will see some more examples of how to do this.

Pie charts: In a pie chart all (100%) of the data is shown in a circle (360°) which is split into sections. Each section represents a numerical proportion. It is a good way to show relative sizes of data and usually the percentage is given next to the 'slice of the pie'.

Pictogram: A pictogram is a chart that uses pictures or symbols to represent a certain number of items. Each symbol has to be the same size with equal gaps between them. Each row should be labelled and a key given.

Venn diagrams: A Venn diagram is a diagram in which data sets and their relationships are represented by circles. The sets of data usually have something in common and this is where the circles will overlap.

An example of each is shown on the next page.

It is important to remember that 360° in a pie chart equals 100%.

DEVELOP

Below is an example of a pie chart, a pictogram and a Venn diagram. See if you can answer the questions relating to each chart.

Survey of 600 Childrens' favourite colours

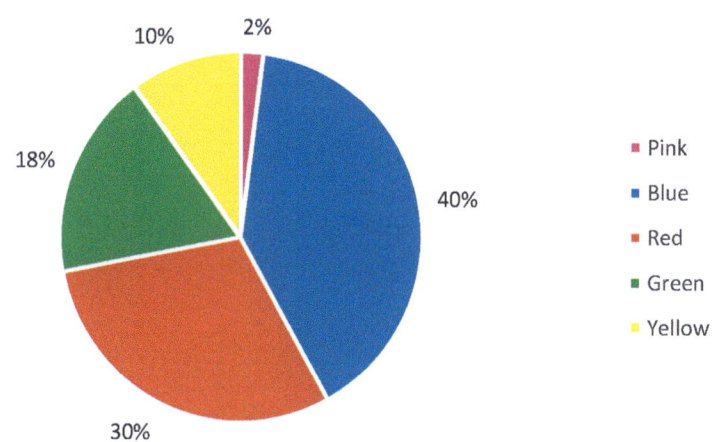

1)   How many children preferred the colour red?
2)   What was the percentage of children whose favourite colour was blue?
3)   What was the angle of the pie slice made up of the children whose favourite colour was yellow?
4)   What was the total number of children who preferred blue and pink?
5)   How many more children liked red than yellow?

Pictogram 1: Children's favourite television programmesm

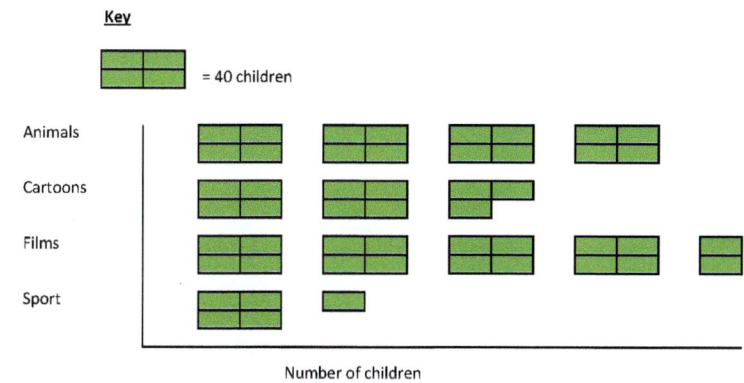

6)   How many children watched animal programmes?
7)   How many more children preferred to watch films than cartoons?
8)   How many children altogether preferred to watch films and sport?
9)   What was the least popular type of programme?
10)   What was the difference between the most and least popular?

DEVELOP

Venn diagram 1: Children's pets in Class 6A

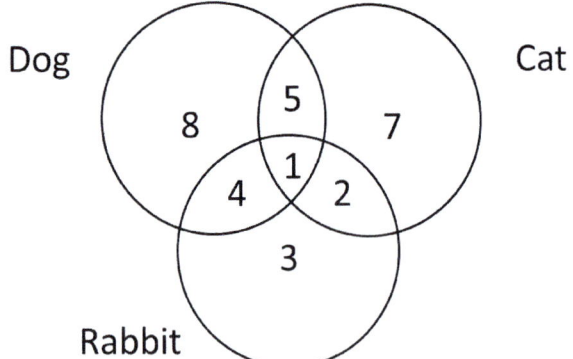

11) How many children have a dog and a rabbit but not a cat?

12) How many children have all types of animals?

13) How many children have a cat and a dog but not a rabbit?

14) How many children are in the class?

15) How many children have either a cat or a rabbit?

A Venn diagram is clever because it shows lots of information.

TIMED TEST   *15 MINS*

Look at the **comparative dual bar chart** below, and answer the following questions.

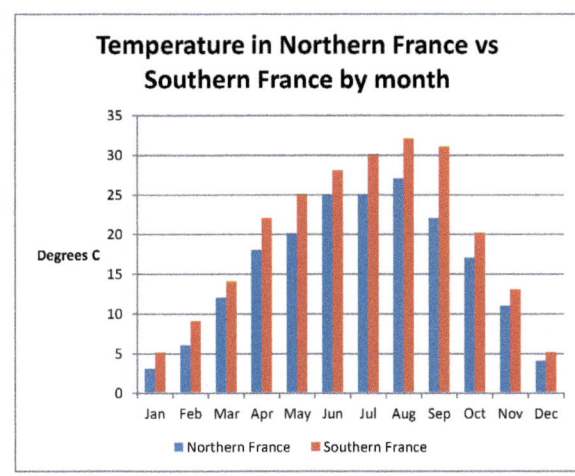

1)   Which is the warmest month to live in southern France?

A	B	C	D	E
Oct	June	Aug	Sept	May

2)   Which two months have same temperature in northern France?

A	B	C	D	E
Jun & Jul	Jan & Dec	Oct & May	Jul & Sept	May & Oct

3)   In which month was the lowest recorded temperature in northern France?

A	B	C	D	E
Aug	Jan	Dec	Sept	Feb

4)   What is the range of temperature in southern France?

A	B	C	D	E
2.5 – 26°	5 – 26°	6 – 30°	4 – 32°	5 – 32°

A bar chart is a good way to compare lots of information.

A conversion chart

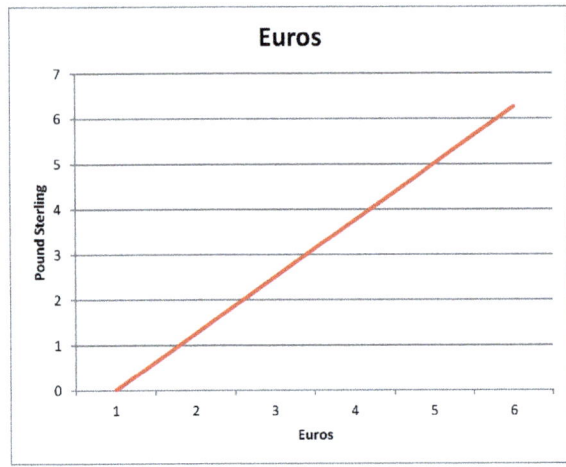

The above conversion graph is used to convert amounts of money between pounds and euros. (The answer is directly above the number on the axis)
Answer the following questions using the graph.

5)   Convert 5 euros to the nearest pound.

A	B	C	D	E
£2	£3	£2.5	£4	£3.10

6)   How many euros is £5?

A	B	C	D	E
8 euros	7 euros	9 euros	7.5 euros	8.5 euro

7)   On holiday in France, a taxi ride cost 15 euros. How much did this cost in pounds?

A	B	C	D	E
£15	£10	£20	£9	£8

Now answer the following questions about the pie chart below.

Top five hobbies

Key	
Football	
Reading	
Computer games	
Dance	
Cooking	

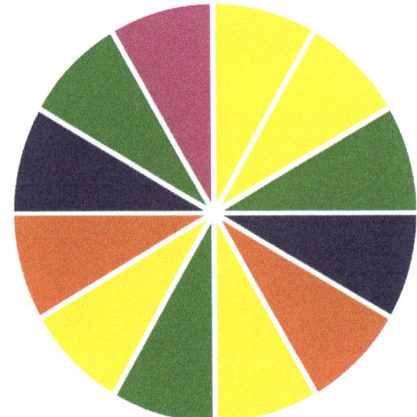

8)   What is the total angle representing dance on the pie chart?

A	B	C	D	E
30°	90°	25°	60°	50°

9)   If 60 children liked reading the most, how many children altogether liked computer games and football the most?

A	B	C	D	E
300	210	360	270	420

10)   What fraction of the children in the survey favoured dance? In its simplest form the fraction should be:

A	B	C	D	E
²⁄₁₂	¼	²⁄₆	⅙	⅓

11)   What percentage of children's favourite hobby was computer games?

A	B	C	D	E
40%	25%	36%	20%	30%

The chart below shows the types of litter collected at the Queen's Jubilee celebration in the local park in 1 day.

Crisp packets	CRISPS	CRISPS	CRISPS	CRISPS	CRIS
Cans	🥫	🥫	🥫		
Bottles	🍾	🍾	🍾	🍾	🍾

Key   = 100 crisp packets   = 100 cans   = 100 bottles

12)   How many bottles were collected in total during the day?

A	B	C	D	E
100	700	500	400	450

13)   How many more crisp packets than cans were collected?

A	B	C	D	E
150	25	100	125	50

14)   How many crisp packets and cans were collected in total?

A	B	C	D	E
675	725	700	750	650

15)   How many items of rubbish were collected in total?

A	B	C	D	E
900	1150	1000	800	1100

Page 42

SECTION 3:
SHAPE AND SPACE

LEARN

Types of angles

In the CEM 11+ exams you will not have any mathematical equipment. Therefore, it is important that you can recognise the main angles as you are unable to use a protractor to measure them. The size of the turn decides the type of angle. Below are some examples of these angles.

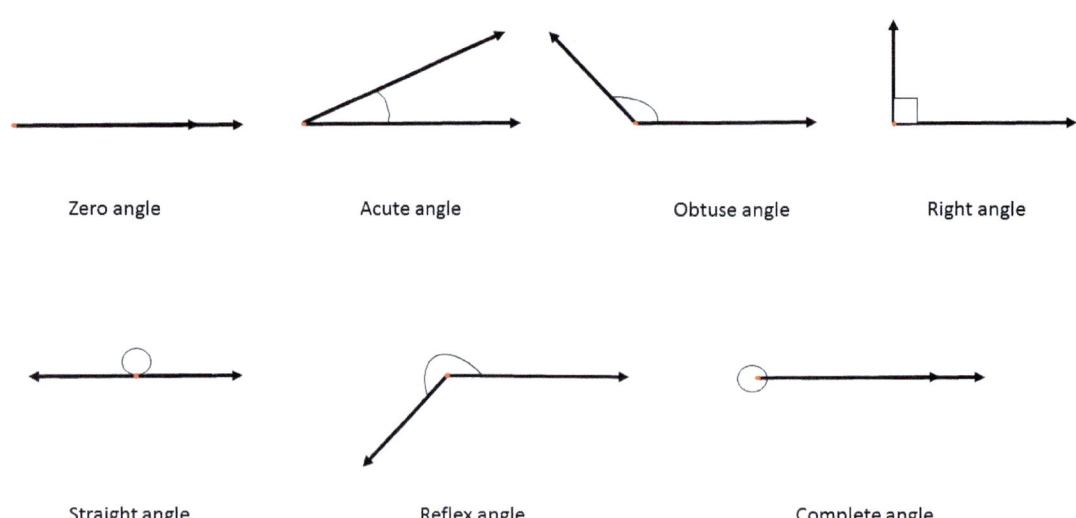

Before doing your exam it is a good idea to learn the main angle names. For example, a question might be, what do we call an angle that is $112°$?

An angle less than (<) 90° is called acute.
An angle more than (>) 90° but less than (<) 180° is called an obtuse angle.
An angle greater than (>) 180° is called a reflex angle.
An angle of 90° is called a right angle.
An angle of 180° cand be called a supplementary angle.

An angle that is $112°$ is between $90°$ and $180°$ so is called obtuse.

Interior angles

The other important facts to remember when learning about angles are the interior angles of different shapes. A very useful formula to help you work out any shape's interior angles is shown below:

$(n - 2) \times 180$ = interior angles of the shape

n = number of sides

LEARN

Example one: Working out the interior angles of a shape

So, if we have a quadrilateral (four-sided shape) we can substitute the n for 4.

$(4 - 2) \times 180 = 360°$

Missing angles
Using simple algebraic equations can help you to work out the angles of many different shapes, as it helps to answer the unknown angle.

Example two: Working out the missing angle in a triangle

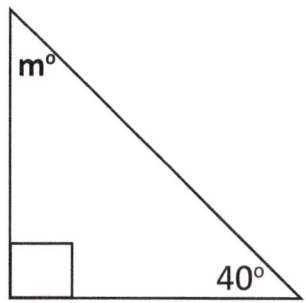

Using the formula for a trangle (three sided shape) calculate $(3 - 2) \times 180 = 180°$ we know the angles of a triangle add up to 180°. By writing out the question in a simple algebraic equation we are able to find the missing angle, m°.

$m° = 180 - (90° + 40°)$

$m° = 180 - 130$

$m° = 50$

The interior angles of all quadrilaterals equal a total of 360º.

DEVELOP

Try these questions below which require a knowledge of angles.

1) What is the name of an angle that is 185°?

2) How many degrees are tere between 12 and 3 on a clock face? And what is this angle called?

3) What is the name of an angle that is 30°?

4) In a regular pentagon, what is the total of the interior angles?

5) What is the name of an angle that is 164°?

6) In a supplementary angle one angle is 17°. What is the other one?

7) In this triangle, how many degrees is angle A°?

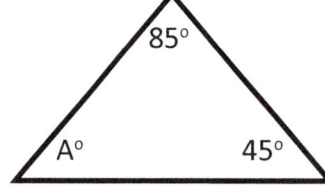

8) What is the value of Q°?

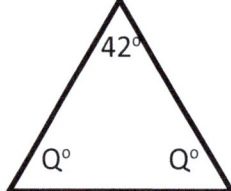

9) Can you work out the value of P° in the circle below?

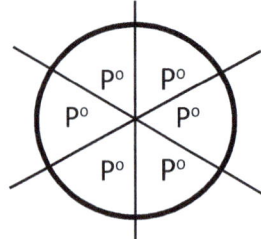

10) What are the angles A° and B°?

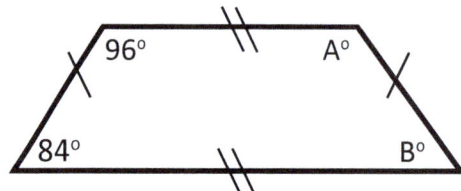

TIMED TEST   15 MINS

1) Two angles on a straight line are 130° and 19°. What is the size of the third angle?

| A | B | C | D | E |
| 31° | 180° | 39° | 90° | 50° |

2) A ship was facing southwest and turned the bow 270° anti-clockwise. Which way is the ship facing now?

| A | B | C | D | E |
| west | south | south east | north east | north west |

3) A shape has eight regular sides. How many degrees is each individual interior angle?

| A | B | C | D | E |
| 360° | 135° | 10° | 45° | 18° |

4) If Zak faces northwest and turns 135° clockwise, which way will he be facing?

| A | B | C | D | E |
| south | west | south east | east | north east |

5) Inside a scalene triangle two of the angles are 21° and 67°. What is the size of the third angle?

| A | B | C | D | E |
| 180° | 80° | 90° | 35° | 92° |

6) How many sides does a shape with interior angles totalling 1440° have?

| A | B | C | D | E |
| 14 | 6 | 12 | 8 | 10 |

7) How many degrees between 10 and 2 on a clock face?

| A | B | C | D | E |
| 180° | 150° | 120° | 140° | 110° |

8) Inside an isosceles triangle the top angle is 40°. What is one of the bottom angles?

| A | B | C | D | E |
| 50° | 80° | 70° | 140° | 90° |

9) In the pentagon below, what is the value of M°?

A	B	C	D	E
130°	120°	50°	145°	135°

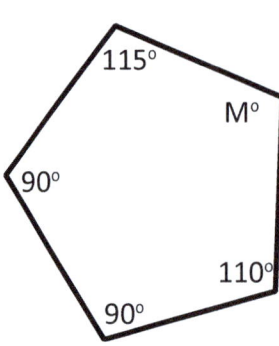

10) What is the value of X°?

A	B	C	D	E
79°	69°	111°	159°	175°

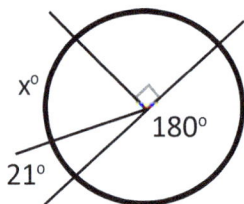

11) Out of the following angles which is a reflex angle?

A	B	C	D	E
79°	37°	202°	179°	150°

12) One angle measures 35°. What is its supplementary angle?

A	B	C	D	E
325°	145°	55°	100°	155°

13) A boat turns its rudder 55°. What would be its complementary angle?

A	B	C	D	E
100°	45°	90°	35°	145°

14) Inside a kite there are three angles measuring 95°, 95° and 58°. What is the fourth angle?

A	B	C	D	E
125°	115°	95°	114°	112°

15) A car windscreen has two angles of 72°. What are the other two angles combined?

A	B	C	D	E
90°	216°	218°	72°	145°

LEARN

In the 11+ exams you may be asked questions about 2D shapes. 2D shapes are sometimes called **polygons**. All the sides of a regular polygon are the same length and all the angles are equal. All other polygons are irregular. It is important to be able to recognise the common 2D shapes and also know their **properties**.

Below are some pictures of common 2D shapes. Can you match the names to the shape?

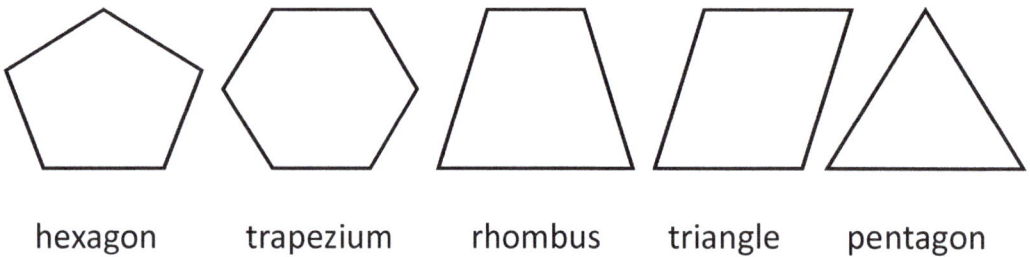

| hexagon | trapezium | rhombus | triangle | pentagon |

We are surrounded by shapes in everyday life and it is fun looking for certain shapes, for example different shaped windows and exploring properties of different shapes, for example how many right angles are inside your front door. When describing shapes we often use the following words: vertices, pairs of parallel sides, perpendicular sides and angles.

This table shows the properties of some 2D shapes.

Name of shape	Vertices (corners)	Pairs of parallel sides	Perpendicular sides
square	4	2	2
rectangle	4	2	2
trapezium	4	1	0
kite	4	0	0
oval (ellipse)	0	0	0
pentagon	5	0	0
regular hexagon	6	3	0

DEVELOP

All the following questions relate to 2D shapes.

1) How many sides does an ellipse have?

2) How many parallel sides does a parallelogram have?

3) Can you name five quadrilaterals?

(i)
(ii)
(iii)
(iv)
(v)

4) A 50p coin is based on which polygon?

5) Which of the following shapes is irregular?

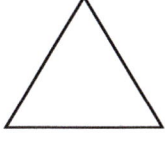 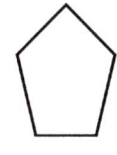 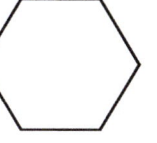 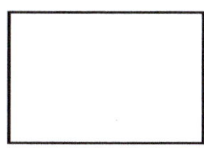

    A   B   C   D

6) How many pairs of parallel sides does a parallelogram have?

7) How many equal sides does a rhombus have?

8) How many sides does a decagon have?

9) What is a nine-sided shape called?

10) What is the following shape called?

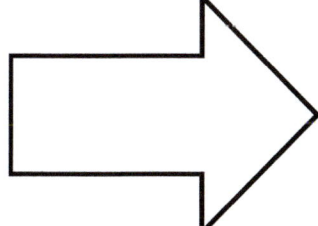

LEARN

Recognising 3D shapes and being able to name them is important. Can you name these common 3D shapes?

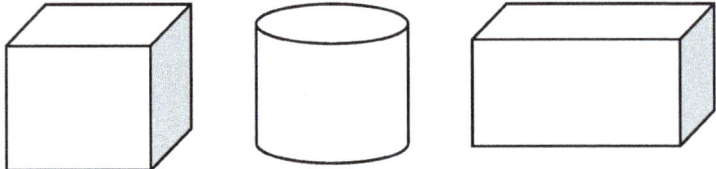

When describing 3D shapes you must use the correct terminology. By using the diagram below match up the words on the left with the correct definitions.

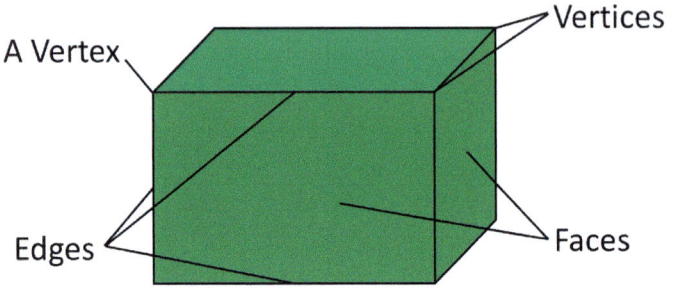

Vertices (vertex)   where two faces meet on a solid 3D shape.

Edges   points or corners on a solid 3D shape.

Faces   the flat parts on a solid 3D shape.

Being able to describe the features of any 3D shape is important.

DEVELOP

Now try to answer these questions about 3D shapes.

1) How many vertices does a triangular prism have?

2) How many faces does a cylinder have?

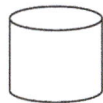

3) What is the total number of edges of a cube and cuboid added together?

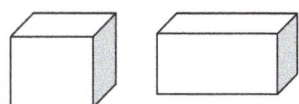

4) How many faces does a tetrahedron have?

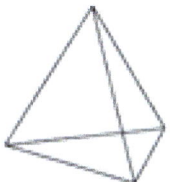

5) Total the number of vertices of a pentagonal prism and a square-based pyramid.

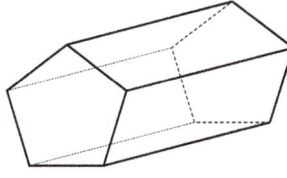 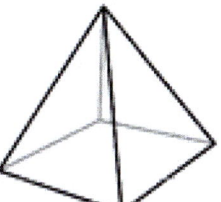

6) Multiply the vertices on a sphere by the faces on a hexagonal prism.

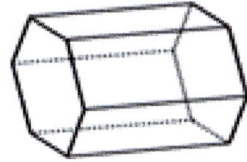 

DEVELOP

7)   How many faces has a cone?

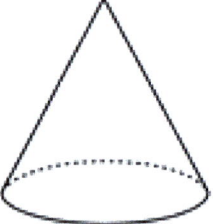

8)   How many faces has a dodecahedron?

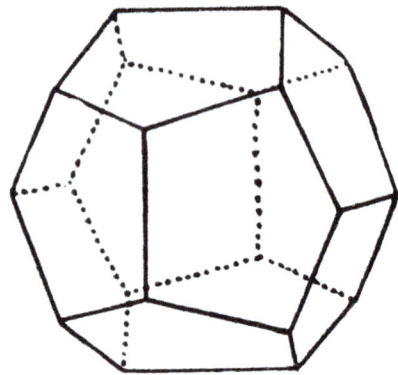

9)   How many edges does a square-based pyramid have?

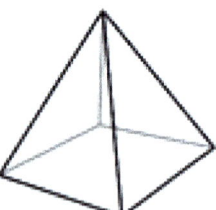

10)   What is the name of a 3D shape which has two edges, three faces and no vertices?

TIMED TEST   15 MINS

1)   Which of the following lines are parallel?

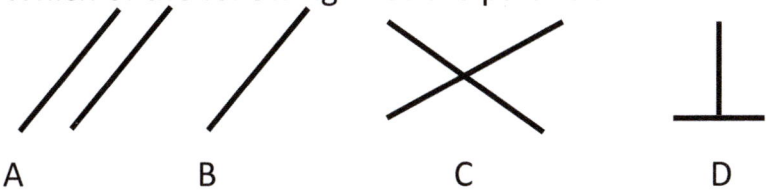

A   B   C   D

2)   What is the sum of the sides of a nonagon and decagon?
A   B   C   D
11   18   19   21

3)   A triangle has the following three angles 95˚, 11˚ and 74˚. What is the name of this type of triangle?
A   B   C   D
isosceles   scalene   right angle   equilateral

4)   What is the order of rotational symmetry of a square?

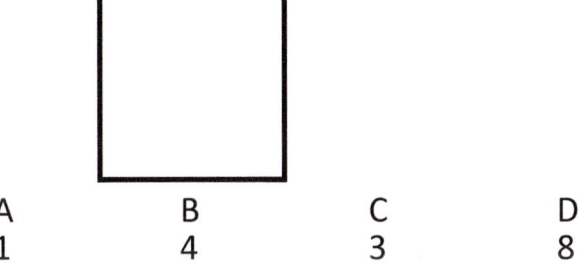

A   B   C   D
1   4   3   8

5)   Can you complete the following passage?

equal	rectangle	ninety	diagonals	sides	parallel	four

A .... has .... equal .... The angles are all .... and the
.... are equal. Each angle is .... degrees. This shape is sometimes called an oblong. It has two sets of .... sides.

6)   Multiply the number of vertices a heptagon has by the number of edges an octagon has.
A   B   C   D
63   54   56   64

7)   Which shape is a quadrilateral?

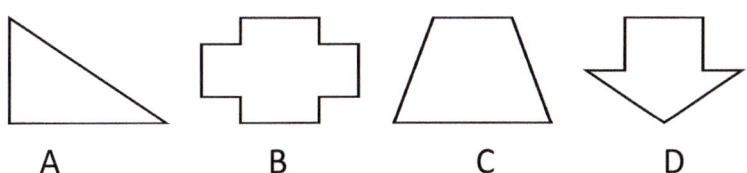

A   B   C   D

8) Divide the number of sides a nonagon has by the number of sides a scalene triangle has.

A	B	C	D
2	6	9	3

9) Which of the following shapes has eight sides?

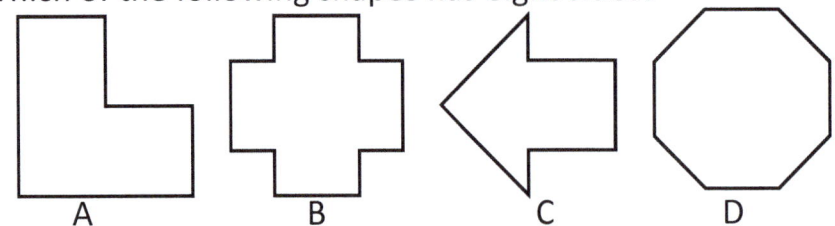

A   B   C   D

10) Which of the following lines are perpendicular?

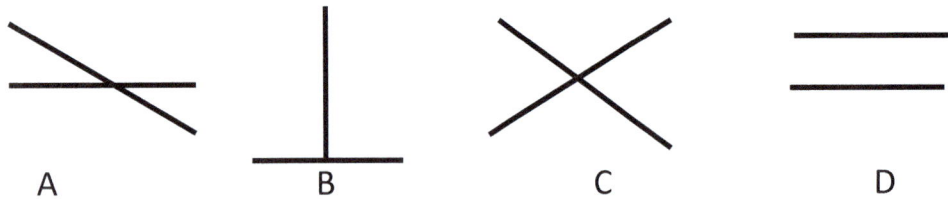

A   B   C   D

11) Zoe has a box of chocolates. How many faces and vertices does it have?

A	B	C	D	E
14	10	16	8	20

12) John's pencil holder on his desk is a hexagonal prism. How many vertices does it have?

A	B	C	D	E
10	16	5	12	4

13) Multiply the number of faces a cone has by the number of faces a triangular prism has.

A	B	C	D	E
3	10	6	14	8

14) What is the name of this shape when the net is folded up?

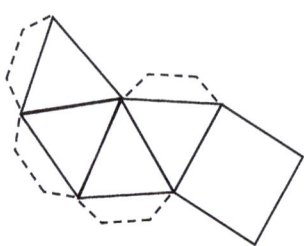

A	B	C	D
hemisphere	sphere	cube	square-based pyramid

15) How many hemispheres are required to make six spheres?

A	B	C	D	E
2	24	12	6	8

Lesson 11: Perimeter and Area

LEARN

Often these two keywords can be forgotten or muddled up. Let's make sure you've remembered the difference between these measurements.

Perimeter: This is the total distance round the edge of a 2D shape. It can be measured in mm, cm, m and km.

Area: This is the space inside the perimeter and can be counted in square units. It can be measured in mm^2, cm^2, m^2 or km^2.

Example one: Finding the perimeter of a 2D shape
To find the perimeter of a 2D shape you must add together all the side lengths. Below is a diagram which shows how to calculate the perimeter.

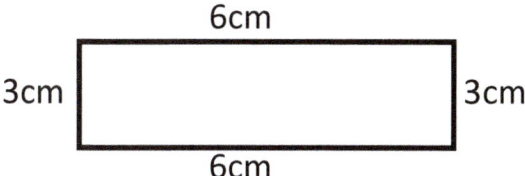

P = 6cm + 3cm + 6cm + 3cm = 18cm

Using a dot or eliminating each line as the sides are added together can help prevent missing an edge or counting a side again.

When calculating the perimeter of a rectangle you can use the following formula:

P = 2 (L + W) P is the perimeter, L is the length and W is the width of the rectangle.

Example two: Finding the area of a 2D shape
To find the area of a common shape you multiply the sides together. So, if a square has sides of 7cm you can simply multiply 7cm by 7cm to give $49cm^2$. A simple formula can also be written to find the area of a rectangle.

A = L × W   A is the area, L is the length and W is the width of the rectangle.
And here is another example:

2cm	1	2	3	4	5	6	7	8
	9	10	11	12	13	14	15	16

8cm

A = 8cm × 2cm = $16cm^2$

LEARN

Below are the formulae for finding the areas of triangles, parallelograms and trapeziums. As for tasks involving angles, you can use simple algebraic expressions to help answer questions on shapes.

Triangle: A = ½base × height

Parallelogram: A = base × height

Trapezium: A = ½(A + b)h.

DEVELOP

1) What is the perimeter of a rectangle that measures 6m by 2m?

2) Find the area of a square which measures 9cm.

3) The total perimeter of a square is 28cm. What is the length of one side?

4) Calculate the area of a rectangle with a length of 15cm and a width of 6cm.

5) If a regular hexagon has sides of 8cm, what is the perimeter?

6) Find the perimeter of this triangle.

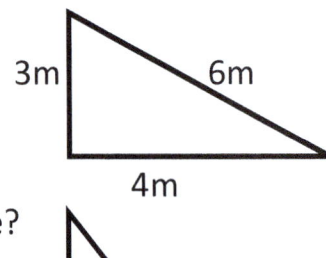

7) What is the area of this triangle?

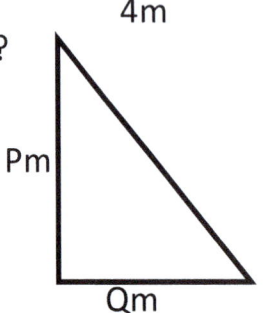

DEVELOP

8) If the side of a regular hexagon is W and the perimeter is 48cm, what is the value of W?

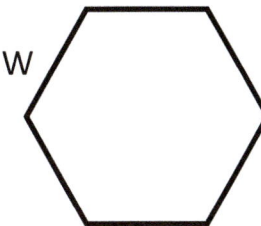

9) The area of this rectangle is 50cm², so what is the value of w?

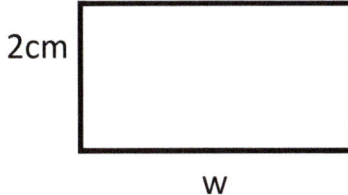

10) The area of this square is 9cm², so what is the value of t?

The perimeter of a shape is the total distance around its edge. The area is the two-dimensional space it covers.

TIMED TEST   15 MINS

1) Find the area of a square whose perimeter is 24cm.

A	B	C	D	E
72cm²	64cm²	16cm²	36cm²	48cm²

2) If the area of a rectangle is 60cm and the length is 10cm, what is the width?

A	B	C	D	E
6cm	10cm	12cm	4cm	8cm

3) What is the perimeter of a rectangle with a width of 7cm and a length of 11cm?

A	B	C	D	E
28cm	36cm	44cm	50cm	77cm

4) What is the area of a square with sides of length 12m?

A	B	C	D	E
136m²	168m²	140m²	144m²	150m²

5) What is the perimeter of a heptagon which has sides 9cm long?

A	B	C	D	E
72cm	54cm	80cm	63cm	60cm

6) Find the perimeter of this triangle.

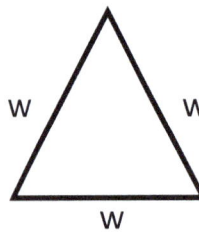

A	B	C	D	E
w³	3w + w	w + w + w	w²	w + w

7) What is the area of this triangle?

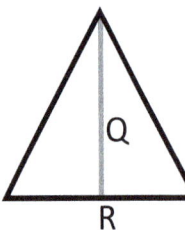

A	B	C	D	E
R+Q	QR	(½ R)Q	(½ Q)R	½ QR

8) If W is 4, what is the area?

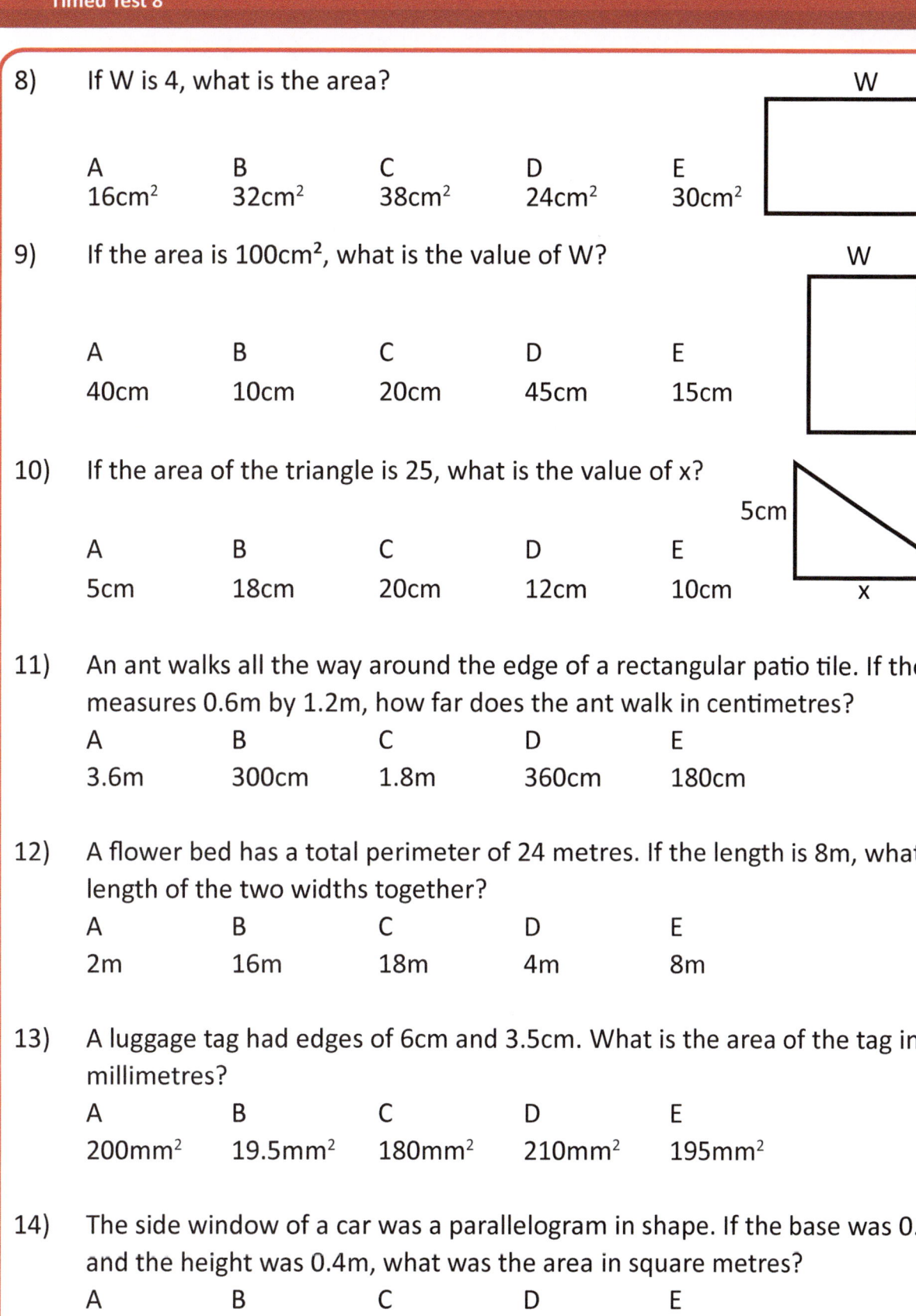

A	B	C	D	E
16cm²	32cm²	38cm²	24cm²	30cm²

9) If the area is 100cm², what is the value of W?

A	B	C	D	E
40cm	10cm	20cm	45cm	15cm

10) If the area of the triangle is 25, what is the value of x?

A	B	C	D	E
5cm	18cm	20cm	12cm	10cm

11) An ant walks all the way around the edge of a rectangular patio tile. If the tile measures 0.6m by 1.2m, how far does the ant walk in centimetres?

A	B	C	D	E
3.6m	300cm	1.8m	360cm	180cm

12) A flower bed has a total perimeter of 24 metres. If the length is 8m, what is the length of the two widths together?

A	B	C	D	E
2m	16m	18m	4m	8m

13) A luggage tag had edges of 6cm and 3.5cm. What is the area of the tag in millimetres?

A	B	C	D	E
200mm²	19.5mm²	180mm²	210mm²	195mm²

14) The side window of a car was a parallelogram in shape. If the base was 0.5m long and the height was 0.4m, what was the area in square metres?

A	B	C	D	E
2m²	0.2m²	1m²	0.4m²	4m²

15) Amy has a rectangular rose garden that measures 8m by 12.5m. One bag of fertilizer can cover 16m². How many bags will she need to cover the rose garden?

A	B	C	D	E
8	3	5	7	9

LEARN

Volume

The volume of a solid 3D object is the amount of space it takes up. To find the volume of a cube or cuboid you multiply together the length (L), width (W) and height (H). This can be represented as L × W × H.

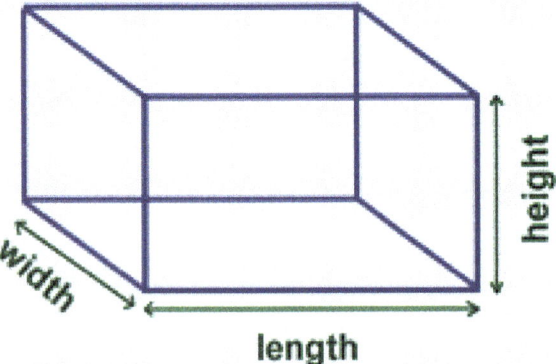

Therefore, if we calculate the volume (cm³) of a cuboid which has 9cm in length, 5cm in width and 8cm in height L × W × H would be the method.

9cm × 5cm × 8cm = 360cm³

Capacity

The capacity is the amount of liquid or water a container can hold. You measure capacity in litres (L) or millilitres (ml).

To help solve capacity questions it is useful to know simple equivalent values. Can you complete the table below? Lesson 4 will also help you with conversions.

Container	Litres	Millilitres
Bucket	8 litres	
Water bottle	1 litre	
Bottle of juice	0.5L	
Mug of coffee	0.3L	
Cup of tea	0.2L	
1 teaspoon of medicine	0.025L	

Another important measure of capacity is centilitres (cL or cl). This is a metric unit of volume that is equal to one hundredth of a litre.

DEVELOP

Use your knowledge of volume and capacity to answer the following questions.

Volume
What is the volume of the following cubes and cuboids?

1)   3cm × 7cm × 5cm =

2)   4cm × 2cm × 8cm =

3)   6cm × 6cm × 6cm =

4)   10cm × 20cm × 40cm =

5)   0.5m × 0.4m × 0.6m =

Capacity
Convert the following amounts into equivalent values.

6)   How many millilitres in 1.3 litres?

7)   Convert 2400ml into litres.

8)   What is 300ml in centilitres?

9)   How many 25ml will be needed to fill a 400ml bottle?

10)   How many millilitres in 9 centilitres?

A shape's volume is the measure of its total three-dimensional space.

TIMED TEST   15 MINS

1) What is the volume of cube which measures 4m in height?

A	B	C	D	E
16m³	32m³	64m³	24m³	72m³

2) Find the missing measurement in this volume calculation.

9cm × ? × 3cm = 135cm³

A	B	C	D	E
5cm	3cm	6cm	7cm	8cm

3) The length of a cuboid is 21cm and the width is 10cm. If the volume is 4200cm³, what is the height?

A	B	C	D	E
30cm	40cm	10cm	20cm	50cm

4) What is the volume of a cuboid with the following measurements?

L 6cm   W 3.5cm   H 3cm

A	B	C	D	E
53cm³	60cm³	58cm³	55cm³	63cm³

5) A small box has the following measurements: 5cm length, 0.15m width and 60mm height. Work out the volume in millimetres cubed (mm³).

A	B	C	D	E
4500mm³	450000mm³	4.5mm³	200mm³	300mm³

6) If a bottle holds 2 litres and 300ml are poured out, how much is left in the bottle in millilitres?

A	B	C	D	E
700ml	1700ml	900ml	1600ml	2300ml

7) A flask of tea holds 1 litre. If each cup holds approximately 200ml, how many cups can be made from three flasks?

A	B	C	D	E
16	14	15	13	17

8) A full bottle holds 1.75 litres of lemonade. If three identical glasses holding 300ml each are filled with lemonade, how much is left in the bottle in litres?

A	B	C	D	E
0.85L	0.75L	0.65L	0.5L	0.35L

9) The width of a room is 5m and its length is 10m. What is the height if the total volume of the room is 100m^3?

A	B	C	D	E
10m	20m	2m	2.5m	10m

10) A bath has a volume of 2.5m^3. What are the dimensions of the bath?

A
2m × 0.50m × 0.5m

B
1.5m × 1m × 1m

C
1m × 1.5m × 2.5m

D
3m × 2m × 1m

E
1m × 1m × 2.5m

11) What is the volume of this cuboid?

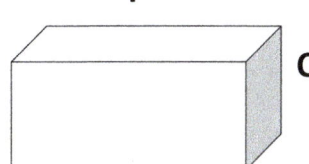

A	B	C	D	E
PQR	QR	P+Q+R	R+Q	PQ

12) The volume of a box is 120cm^3. What is the value of T?

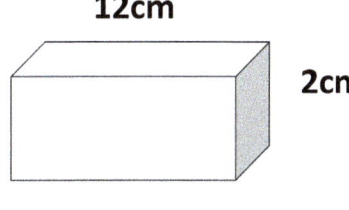

A	B	C	D	E
10cm	8cm	3cm	2cm	5cm

13)   If a cuboid has a volume of 450cm³, what is the value of e?

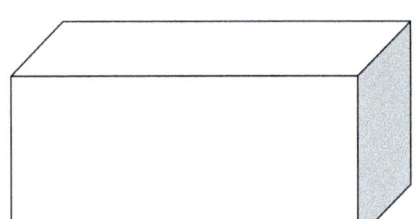

A	B	C	D	E
100cm	250cm	15cm	10cm	25cm

14)   If the volume of the cube is 8cm³, what is the value of P?

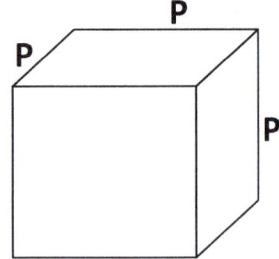

A	B	C	D	E
8cm	2cm	4cm	6cm	3cm

15)   If a swimming pool is 25m long, 10m wide and 2m deep, how many litres of water can it hold if 1 cubic metre equals 1000 litres?

A	B	C	D	E
100000L	500000L	50000L	10000L	5000L

SECTION 4:
GLOSSARY AND ANSWERS

Glossary

BIDMAS:	Stands for brackets, indices, division, multiplication, addition and subtraction, i.e. the order in which a calculation is carried out.
Brackets:	Symbols that show those terms that should be treated together and calculated first, in the order of operations.
Capacity:	The measure of the space within a 3D object.
Continuous data:	Data that comes from measurement such as rainfall measurement.
Consecutive:	One number following the other continuously.
Cube number:	A cube number is a number which has been produced by another number that has been multiplied by itself and itself again, e.g. $3 \times 3 \times 3 = 27$. It is a whole number that has been raised to the power of 3.
Cumulative frequency:	A running sum of the frequencies.
Data:	Collective name for pieces of information, often used for reference or analysis.
Decimal place:	The position of a digit to the right of a decimal point.
Decimal point:	In a decimal number the decimal point separates the whole number from the part that is smaller than 1
Denominator:	The number at the bottom of a fraction.
Density:	The mass per unit volume of a solid.
Digit:	Any of the numerals from 0 to 9, especially when forming part of a number.
Discrete data:	Data that can be counted such as number of house points collected in a week.
Equation:	Has an equals sign in it, e.g. $3x + 1 = 7$
Estimate:	Roughly calculate or judge the value, number or quantity.
Exchange:	To 'borrow' in subtraction.
Expression:	A collection of terms or variables, e.g. $2x + 2y$ or $5r + 6$ without an equals sign.
Factor:	A number or quantity that when multiplied with another produces a given number or expression.
Formula:	A mathematical relationship or rule expressed in symbols. The plural is formulae.
Fraction:	A numerical quantity that is not a whole number.
Frequency:	The number of times an event occurs.
Frequency chart:	A table that shows the total for each category or group of data.
Imperial system:	A measuring system based on the foot, gallons, and pounds as units of length, capacity and weight or mass.
Index (power):	The index of a number says how many times to use the number in multiplication. It is written as a small number to the right and above the base number. In this example: $4^3 = 4 \times 4 \times 4 = 64$. The plural of index is indices.
Integer:	A whole number.
Intervals:	An interval is the distance between one number and the next on the scale of a graph.
Length:	The distance of the longest dimension of a shape.
Linear:	A straight line on a graph.
Line graph:	Graph formed by joining points together with straight lines.
Mass:	The weight of an object. A measure of how much matter is in an object. Mass is measured in grams and kilograms in the metric system and in pounds and stones in the imperial system.

Metric system:	The decimal measuring system based on the metre, litre and gram as units of length, capacity and weight or mass. Converted in powers of 10
Multiples:	The numbers in multiplication tables, e.g. multiples of 3 are: 3, 6, 9, 12, etc.
Numerator:	The number above the line in a fraction showing how many parts.
Place value:	The numerical value that a digit has by virtue of its position in a number.
Power of:	The power of a number says how many times to use the number in a multiplication. It is written as a small number to the right and above the base number.
Prime number:	A number that only has two factors: itself and 1
Product:	The result when two numbers are multiplied together.
Quotient:	A result obtained by dividing one quantity by another.
Regroup:	Regrouping is often used in subtraction and addition. It is also known as 'carrying', 'exchanging' and 'borrowing' numbers.
Rounding:	Alteration of a number to one that is less exact but more convenient for calculations.
Sequence:	A set of numbers containing a pattern.
Significant figures:	Each of the digits of a number that are used to express it to the required degree of accuracy, starting from the first non zero digit.
Square number:	A square number is a number that results from a number that has been multiplied by itself e.g. $2 \times 2 = 4$. It is a whole number that has been raised to the power of 2
Substitution:	The act of replacing a letter with a number or a number with a letter.
Tabulated:	To put information into a table format.
Tally chart:	A table with tally marks to show a valuable data set.
Term:	One of the parts of an expression or a number in a number sequence.
Triangular number:	Like square numbers which can be illustrated in a square pattern, you can illustrate triangular numbers in two types of triangle patterns.
Vertices:	A corner on a shape is referred to as a vertex. The plural is vertices.
Volume:	The amount of space that a substance or object occupies, or that is enclosed within a container.

Answers

Lesson 1: Ratio and Proportion page 8

Develop page 10

1)	3:5	4)	1:50	7)	4:1	10)	1:4
2)	6:4	5)	10:3	8)	8:7
3)	7:2	6)	3:1	9)	9:7

Timed Test 1 page 11

Question	Answer	Explanation
1	B = 80p	3 + 2 + 1 = 6 'equal parts'. Divide £2.40 by 6 to work out one part of the ratio = £0.40. Daisy had a ratio of 2. 2 × £0.40 = 80p
2	D = 30	5 + 3 + 1 = 9 'equal parts'. Divide 54 sweets by 9 to work out one part of the ratio = 6. Arzaan had a ratio of 5. 5 × 6 = 30
3	C = £600	2 + 3 = 5 'equal parts'. Divide £1000 by 5 to work out one part of the ratio = £200. Kushi had a ratio of 3. 3 × £200 = £600
4	E = 63	7 + 3 = 10 'equal parts'. Divide 90 beads by 10 to work out one part of the ratio = 9. Silver has a ratio of 7. 7 × 9 = 63
5	A = 500000	1cm = 100km. 5 × 100km = 500km. Multiply 500km by 1000 to convert into metres = 500,000m
6	D = 8	4 + 2 + 1 = 7 'equal parts'. Divide 14 orange segments by 7 to work out one part of the ratio = 2. The largest share has a ratio of 4, therefore 4 × 2 = 8
7	B = 8	7 + 4 + 2 = 13 'equal parts'. Divide 52 playing cards by 13 to work out one part of the ratio = 4. The smallest share has a ratio of 2, therefore 4 × 2 = 8
8	C = 36	2 + 3 + 1 = 6 'equal parts'. Divide 108 biscuits by 6 to work out one part of the ratio = 18. Two parts of the ratio is 18 × 2 = 36
9	E = 240	3 + 2 + 2 = 7 'equal parts'. Divide 560 runs by 7 to work out one part of the ratio = 80. Freddie had a ratio of 3, therefore 80 × 3 = 240
10	B = 20	1 + 4 + 2 + 1 + 3 = 11 'equal parts'. Divide 55 cars by 11 to work out one part of the ratio = 5. The ratio for red cars was 4, therefore 4 × 5 = 20
11	C = 1.5m	1cm = 30cm of the model train. 5cm × 30cm = 150cm. To convert into metres, divide by 100. 150 ÷ 100 = 1.5m
12	A = 48	1 + 2 + 3 + 4 + 1 + 1 = 12 'equal parts'. Divide 144 sweets by 12 to work out one part of the ratio = 12. The greatest proportion of sweets was a ratio of 4, therefore 4 × 12 = 48
13	D = 67.5km	1cm = 9km on the map. 7.5 × 9 = 67.5cm
14	B = 150L	3 + 5 = 8 'equal parts'. Divide 240 litres by 8 to work out one part of the ratio = 30L. 5 parts of water was added, therefore 30L × 5 = 150L
15	D = 30	70 – 10 (for Kajol) = 60, ⅓ of 60 = 20 (for Ragan), 6 + 2 = 8 'equal parts'. Divide the remaining 40 sweets by 8 to work out one part of the ratio = 5 sweets. Dad gets 6 parts, 5 × 6 = 30 sweets

Lesson 2: Probability page 14

Develop page 15
1) $\frac{3}{6}$
2) $\frac{1}{4}$
3) $\frac{1}{2}$
4) $\frac{1}{7}$
5) $\frac{2}{10}$
6) $\frac{5}{12}$
7) $\frac{1}{12}$
8) $\frac{1}{2}$
9) $\frac{3}{4}$
10) $\frac{11}{12}$

Timed Test 2 page16

Question	Answer	Explanation
1	D = $\frac{3}{4}$	There are 8 balls altogether (5 + 2 + 1). Add the red and white balls together, 1 + 5 = 6. Therefore 6 out of 8 = $\frac{3}{4}$
2	C = $\frac{4}{7}$	There are now 7 balls altogether after a white ball has been removed (4 + 2 + 1). The chance of picking a white ball is $\frac{4}{7}$
3	A = $\frac{1}{13}$	There are 4 aces in a pack of cards. $\frac{4}{52}$ at its lowest form is $\frac{1}{13}$
4	D = $\frac{12}{52}$	Altogether there are 12 picture cards (3 pictures × 4 suits). As a probability it is $\frac{12}{52}$
5	C = $\frac{1}{52}$	There is only King of Diamonds, so it has only 1 chance of being selected from the 52 cards
6	B = $\frac{1}{3}$	There are 3 slow songs and 2 house tunes, so 5 songs combined. $\frac{5}{15}$ can be simplified to $\frac{1}{3}$
7	E = $\frac{11}{15}$	15 songs altogether minus 4 hip hop songs is $\frac{11}{15}$
8	D = $\frac{1}{18}$	There are 36 pencils altogether (5 + 2 + 8 + 15 + 6) with 2 blue pencils. $\frac{2}{36}$ can be simplified to $\frac{1}{18}$. The information about the new box is redundant.
9	B = $\frac{7}{36}$	The total of red and blue pencils is 7 (2 + 5) and there are 36 pencils in total
10	E = $\frac{3}{13}$	As 10 black pencils have been lost there are now 26 pencils (36 – 10). The probability of choosing a green pencil is $\frac{6}{26}$ which can be simplified to $\frac{3}{13}$
11	A = 50	The defective rate of calculators is $\frac{1}{20}$. Divide 1000 calculators by 20 which is 50
12	C = certain	It is certain to be a green ball as there is only 1 yellow ball which has already been taken out
13	D = $\frac{5}{6}$	36 chocolates minus 6 milk chocolates leaves 30 dark chocolates. $\frac{30}{36}$ simplified is $\frac{5}{6}$
14	B = $\frac{1}{3}$	There are 6 possible outcomes so the probability of two coins landing heads up is $\frac{2}{6}$. This can be simplified to $\frac{1}{3}$
15	B = $\frac{1}{1296}$	There are a possible 1296 outcomes (6 × 6 × 6 × 6). Therefore the probability of throwing 4 ones is $\frac{1}{1296}$

Answers

Lesson 3: Averages page 18

Develop page 19

1)   20
2)   15
3)   12
4)   15
5)   15.5

Timed Test 3 page 20

Question	Answer	Explanation
1	E = 5km	The total distance covered was 30km and Ankush recorded 6 running journeys, therefore 30 ÷ 6 = 5km
2	D = 400ml	The total is 2000ml, therefore 2000 divided by 5 gives 400ml
3	A = 6kg	The total weight of John's pets is 36kg and he has 6 pets, therefore 36 ÷ 6 = 6kg
4	E = 17	When the hat sales are reordered 12, 14, 17, 32, 47 the middle number is 17
5	C = £3.50	The range is the difference between £4.75 and £1.25 which equals £3.50
6	C = 52mins	The total length of time of the programmes is 260 minutes. Therefore 260 divided by 5 is 52 minutes
7	A = £3	The total cost of the DVD's is £15 and if this amount is divided by 5 it gives £3
8	D = 1010ft	If you reorder these amounts from the smallest to the largest the middle number is 1010ft
9	C = 30000	The total number of tickets sold was 150000 and if this is divided by 5 performances it equals an average of 30000
10	B = 28°C	To work out the range find the difference between the highest and lowest temperatures 21° and −7°, to get the answer 28°C
11	C = 90kg	To work out the average weight divide 630kg by 7, which equals 90kg
12	B = 5.5	If you reorder these amounts from the smallest to the largest the middle number is 5.5
13	D = 283	To work out the mean you need to add all the pages up, 227 + 103 + 258 + 386 + 441 = 1415. Divide the total by 5 books. 1415 ÷ 5 = 283
14	A = £5.31	To work out the range take the highest amount, £6.70, and take away £1.39 to give the answer £5.31
15	D = 195	Multiply 5 by 180 = 900. Now take away the numbers you already have from 900. 900 − 155 − 162 − 190 − 198 = 195. The fifth number is 195

Lesson 4: Conversion page 22

Develop page 24

Metric conversion		Time conversion	
1)	38400cm	11)	108 months
2)	9.8kg	12)	1800 years
3)	27.3L	13)	24 minutes
4)	800cm	14)	120 years
5)	980mm	15)	7000 years
6)	9700m	16)	420 minutes
7)	700ml	17)	36000 seconds
8)	70gs	18)	744 hours
9)	42cm	19)	12600 seconds
10)	7000mm	20)	2922 (includes two leap years)

Timed Test 4 page 25

Question	Answer	Explanation
1	B = 120	6 × 1000 = 6000 ÷ 50ml = 120
2	E = 5040 mins	7 × 3 × 4 × 60 = 5040. 21 × 4 = 84 × 60 = 5040
3	A = 10.5km	3.5 × 3000 = 10500m ÷ 1000 = 10.5km
4	C = 219144 hrs	6 × 366 (leap years every 4 years) × 24 = 52704 19 × 365 × 24 = 166440 52704 + 166440 = 219144 hours
5	E = 4.8km	4 metre = 1 sec × 60 = 240m in 1 min. 240m × 20 = 4800m in 20 min
6	A = 5040 mins	3.5 × 24 = 84 hours × 60 = 5040 minutes
7	B = 1500g	1 box = 10 tins = 15 kg. 1500 ÷ 10 = 1500g
8	C = 6.7km	240000cm ÷ 100 to get to metres = 2400m run 800 m swim 3.5km = 3500 m cycle 6700m: to convert to km ÷ 1000 = 6.7km
9	A = 0.4kg	4 × 1.5kg = 6kg = 6000g ÷ 15 = 400g = 0.4kg
10	B = 4750ml	4.75L × 1000 = 4750
11	C = 1500	25 min × 60 = 1500 sec
12	D = 68000g	17 × 4 × 1000 = 68000g
13	B = 214.76m	1yd = 0.91m × 236 = 214.76
14	D = £72.90	1 gallon = 4.5 litres. 15 gallons = 67.5 litres 67.5 litres × £1.08 = £72.90
15	A = 9	1 acre = ⅗ hectare 15 ÷ 5 = 3 × 3 = 9 15 acres = 9 hectares

Lesson 5: Bar charts 28

Develop page 32

1)   104
2)   30 shops
3)   Town 3
4)   15 shops
5)   46 shops

Lesson 6: Line Graphs page 33

Develop page 35

1)   Friday
2)   Monday and Sunday
3)   Tuesday
4)   42.5 hours
5)   6 hours

Lesson 7: Pie Charts, Pictograms and Venn Diagrams page 36

Develop page 37

1)   180
2)   240
3)   36°
4)   252
5)   120
6)   160 children
7)   70 children
8)   230 children
9)   sport
10)   130
11)   4 children
12)   1 child
13)   5 children
14)   30 children
15)   10 children

Answers

Timed Test 5 page 39

Question	Answer	Explanation
1	C = Aug	August is the warmest month at 32 degrees
2	A = Jun and July	Both June and July have the same temperatures in northern France
3	B = Jan	January had the lowest recorded month at 3 degrees
4	E = 5 – 32°	The range of temperature in southern France is 5 to 32 degrees
5	£3	5 euros converts to £3 on the chart
6	8 euros	£5 converts to 8 euros on the chart
7	£9	We can see that 5 euros equals £3. There are three lots of 5 euros in 15 euros. Then multiply £3 by 3 to give the answer £9
8	D = 60°	The pie chart is divided into 12 sectors. 360° divided by 12 is 30, so each sector is 30°. Two sectors are blue representing dance and so the total angle for dance is 30° + 30°
9	E = 420	Add together the number of children who like computer games (3 sectors) and football (4 sectors). 7 sectors = 7 × 60 = 420 children
10	D = ⅙	2 sectors preferred dance, this equates to ²⁄₁₂. ⅙ is its simplest form
11	B = 25%	3 sectors preferred computer games. This equates to ³⁄₁₂ which is ¼ which is also 25%
12	E = 450	The chart shows 4 and a half bottles. Each bottle equates to 100 that were collected. 4 × 100 = 400 + (100/2) = 450
13	A = 150	425 crisp packets were collected (4 and a quarter packets are in the chart) and 275 cans were collected (2 and ¾ cans are in the chart). The difference is 425 – 275 = 150
14	C = 700	425 crisp packets were collected (4 and a quarter packets are in the chart) and 275 cans were collected (2 and ¾ cans are in the chart). In total 700 items were collected (425 crisp packets + 275 cans)
15	B = 1150	425 crisp packets + 275 cans + 450 bottles = 1150 in total

Lesson 8: Angles page 44

Develop page 46

1) obtuse angle
2) 90° and it is called a rightangle
3) acute angle
4) 540°
5) obtuse angle

6) 163°
7) 50°
8) 69°
9) 60°
10) A = 96° B= 84°

Timed Test 6 page 47

Question	Answer	Explanation
1	A = 31°	Angles on a straight line add up to 180°. Therefore 130° + 19° = 149°, 180° − 149° = 31°
2	E = north west	Turning 270° is the same as three 90° turns. It is important to turn anti-clockwise. The ship will be facing north west
3	B = 135°	The interior angles in a regular octagon total 1080 (n − 2 × 180 = 1080). There are 8 angles, therefore 1080 ÷ 8 = 135°
4	D = east	Turning 135° is the same as 90° + 45° turns. Zak will be facing east
5	E = 92°	The degrees inside a triangle total 180°, therefore 67° + 21° = 88°, 180 − 88° = 92°
6	E = 10	The formula for working out interior angles is (n − 2 × 180 = total interior angles). Therefore, if 10 was the number of sides 10 − 2 × 180 = 1440°
7	C = 120°	Between each number in a clock face there are 30°. There are 4 equal spaces between 10 and 2 moving clockwise, therefore 30 × 4 = 120°
8	C = 70°	Both angles at the base of an isosceles triangle are the same. Take away the angle you know: 180° − 40° equals 140°. 140° divided by 2 = 70°
9	E = 135°	The total degrees inside a pentagon come to 540° (n sides − 2 × 180). If you subtract, 115°, 90°, 90° and 110°, this leaves 135°
10	A = 69°	The straight line totals 180°. A 90° angle is shown plus 21° equals 111°. Therefore 180° − 111° = 69°
11	C = 202°	A reflex angle is greater than 180° therefore 202° is the only option
12	B = 145°	A supplementary angle equals 180°. So, if 180° − 35° = 145°, 145° is the supplementary angle
13	D = 35°	A complementary angle totals 90°. Therefore 90° − 55° = 35°
14	E = 112°	The interior angles of all quadrilaterals total 360°. The given angles total 248° (95° + 95° + 58°). 360° − 248° = 112°
15	B = 216°	A car windscreen is a trapezium so has four sides. So 72° + 72° = 144°. 360° − 144° = 216°

Answers

Lesson 9: 2D shapes page 50

Develop page 51
1) 1
2) 4
3) square, rectangle, kite, trapezium, parallelogram
4) heptagon
5) B
6) 2
7) 4
8) 10
9) nonagon
10) irregular heptagon

Lesson 10: 3D Shapes page 52

Develop page 53
1) 6
2) 3
3) 24
4) 4
5) 15
6) (8×0)
7) 2
8) 12
9) 8
10) cylinder

Timed Test 7 page 55

Question	Answer	Explanation
1	A	Parallel lines do not touch or cross over, therefore B, C and D, are ruled out
2	C = 19	A nonagon has 9 sides and a decagon has 10 sides. 10 + 9 = 19
3	B = scalene	If the angles are all different the triangle is called a scalene
4	B = 4	The order of rotation is 4 because this shape can rotate exactly 4 times on itself
5		A **rectangle** has **four** equal **sides**. The angles are all **equal** and the **diagonals** are equal. Each angle is **ninety** degrees. This shape is sometimes called an oblong. It has two sets of **parallel** sides.
6	C = 56	A heptagon has seven vertices and an octagon has eight sides. 7 × 8 = 56
7	C	All quadrilaterals have four sides. A trapezium is a four-sided shape
8	D = 3	A nonagon is a nine-sided shape and a scalene triangle has three sides. 9 ÷ 3 = 3
9	D	The octagon has eight sides
10	B	Perpendicular lines create a right angle. Therefore, the only option is B
11	A = 14	A box might be a cube or cuboid. Both have six faces and eight vertices. 6 + 8 = 14
12	D = 12	A hexagonal prism has six corners at each end. 6 + 6 = 12
13	B = 10	A cone has two faces and a triangular prism has five. 5 × 2 = 10
14	D = square-based pyramid	The net when folded will create a square-based pyramid
15	C = 12	There are two hemispheres in a sphere. Therefore, 2 × 6 = 12

Lesson 11: Perimeter and Area page 57

Develop page 58
1)   16m
2)   91cm²
3)   7cm
4)   90cm²
5)   48cm
6)   13m
7)   ½(Qm × Pm)
8)   8cm
9)   25cm
10)   3cm

Timed Test 8 page 60

Question	Answer	Explanation
1	D = 36m²	The perimeter is 24cm, therefore each side is 6cm (24 ÷ 4 = 6). To find the area multiply the length by the width, 6 × 6 = 36cm
2	A = 6cm	The area is 60cm. The length is 10cm, so 60cm ÷ 10cm = 6cm. The width is 6cm
3	B = 36cm	The perimeter is 2(L + W), therefore 2 × (7 + 11) = 36cm
4	D = 144m²	The area is L × W, therefore 12m × 12m = 144m²
5	D = 63cm	A heptagon has 7 sides. Each side is 9cm. To find the perimeter multiply 7 × 9 = 63cm
6	C = w+w+w	To solve the perimeter of the triangle you must add together the three sides. Therefore, w + w + w equals the perimeter
7	C = (½R)Q	The area of the isosceles triangle is calculated by ½ base × height therefore (½R) × Q
8	B = 32cm²	W = 4cm. To find the area multiply L × W. 4cm × 8cm = 32cm²
9	C = 20cm	To find the area multiply L × W, so 100cm² divided by 5 = 20cm. W = 20cm
10	E = 10	The area of the rectangle would be 50cm². This would be halved for the triangle to be 25cm². Therefore, the length is 10cm as 10 × 5 = 50cm²
11	D = 360cm	To find the perimeter in metres add together 0.6 + 1.2 × 2 = 3.6m. To convert metres to centimetres multiply by 100. 3.6 × 100 = 360cm
12	E = 8m	Both lengths total 16m. 24m − 16m = 8m. The two widths together total 8m
13	D = 210mm²	The tag has an area of 6cm × 3.5cm = 21cm². To convert centimetres to millimetres multiply 21cm by 10 = 210mm²
14	B = 0.2m²	To find the area of a parallelogram multiply the base by the height. 0.5m × 0.4m = 0.2m²
15	D = 7	To find the area multiply L × W. 8m × 12.5m = 100m². One bag covers 16m². So 100 ÷ 16 = 6.25. Therefore 7 bags are needed

Answers

Lesson 12: Volume and Capacity page 62

Develop page 63
1) 105cm³
2) 64cm³
3) 216cm³
4) 8000cm³
5) 0.12m³
6) 1300ml
7) 2.4L
8) 30cl
9) 16
10) 90ml

Timed Test 9 page 64

Question	Answer	Explanation
1	C = 64m³	Volume is L × W × H, therefore a cube of 4 × 4 × 4 equals 64cm³
2	A = 5cm	To find the missing number multiply the two measurements you have and then divide this into the total volume. 9cm × 3cm = 27cm. 135cm³ divided by 27cm = 5cm
3	D = 20cm	To find the missing number multiply the two measurements you have and then divide this into the total volume. 21cm × 10cm = 210cm. 4200cm³ divided by 210cm = 20cm
4	E = 63cm³	Volume is L × W × H, therefore 6 × 3.5 × 3 equals 63cm³
5	B = 450000 mm³	First convert all measurements to millimetres therefore, 50mm × 150mm × 60mm = 450000mm³
6	B = 1700ml	Convert all measurements to ml (millilitres) before attempting the question. 2000ml − 300ml = 1700ml
7	C = 15	Three flasks equate to 3000ml (3 × 1000ml) 3000ml ÷ 200ml = 15
8	A = 0.85L	Three glasses of lemonade equals 0.9L (300ml × 3). Subtract 0.9L from 1.75L equals 0.85L
9	C = 2m	To find the missing number multiply the two measurements you have and then divide this into the total volume. 5m × 10m = 50m. 100m³ divided by 50m = 2m
10	E = 1m × 1m × 2.5m	1m x 1m x 2.5m = 2.5m³
11	A = PQR	Volume is L × W × H, therefore P × Q × R is the same as PQR
12	E = 5cm	To find the missing number multiply the two measurements you have and then divide this into the total volume. 12cm × 2cm = 24cm. 120cm³ divided by 24cm = 5cm
13	C = 15cm	Divide 450cm³ by 2cm = 225cm. 15cm × 15cm = 225cm
14	B = 2cm	2cm × 2cm × 2cm = 8cm³. P = 2cm
15	B = 500000L	25m × 10m × 2m = 500m. Therefore 500 × 1000L = 500000L

Fill in the tables below with your results from each of the Timed Tests.

Colour the Progress Grid on the next page to see how well you have done.

	Timed Test 1	Timed Test 2	Timed Test 3
Score	/15	/15	/15

	Timed Test 4	Timed Test 5	Timed Test 6
Score	/15	/15	/15

	Timed Test 7	Timed Test 8	Timed Test 9
Score	/15	/15	/15

Colour the grids below with your total mark from each Timed Test to see how well you have done.

Timed Test 1

Timed Test 2

Timed Test 3

Timed Test 4

Timed Test 5

Timed Test 6

Timed Test 7

Timed Test 8

Timed Test 9

Read the statements below for some hints and tips.

0–7: Carefully re-read the 'Learn' section and try the 'Develop' questions again. When you feel confident, retry the Timed Test.

8–12: Good effort, make sure you learn from your mistakes. Review the answers of the questions that you have got wrong and try to understand the correct calculations for next time.

13–15: Well done, you have shown a secure understanding.